FREMONT'S GREATEST WESTERN EXPLORATION

Volume 1: The Dalles to Pyramid Lake

In Fremont's own words.
With modern maps.

P9-CAM-334

John L. Stewart

SET, Inc., Publisher. Vancouver, Washington

FREMONT'S GREATEST WESTERN EXPLORATION.

Volume 1: The Dalles to Pyramid Lake

Copyright © 1999 by John L. Stewart

Library of Congress Catalog Card Number: 99-90758

Manufactured in the United States of America by
Bang Printing, Brainerd, MN

TABLE OF CONTENTS

Author-editor John L. (Larry) Stewart

John started working in 1943 as an 18 year old B-24 bomber navigator flying 31 missions over Germany. He kept a diary from which his first non-technical book was written. After the war he returned to school, then to Jet Propulsion Laboratory where  he helped design the guidance system for the Corporal missile. Again returning to school (Stanford University), he received the Ph.D. in Electrical Engineering, with research on cyclotron resonance. Then came a career as an educator at University of Michigan, California Institute of Technology, University of Southern California, and University of Arizona where he left to become an entrepreneur. While employed as a Professor of Electrical Engineering, he wrote three technical books. His first small company did basic research for the Air Force Bionics program on hearing mechanisms in animals and humans. The research led to hardware and software for early 8-bit personal computers, and later the familiar PC, in the field of speech recording, playback, and word recognition. His company has been called a pioneer in the audio part of the modern multi-media field. Stewart has written many articles, manuals, and analyses, and holds over a dozen patents. Currently retired, he is busier than ever with planned books. He also volunteers as a counselor for SCORE and remains an active private pilot. He and his wife of 48 years, Rita, have two sons and three grandchildren.

ACKNOWLEDGEMENT

An original copy of Fremont's Report to the Congress was inherited. Its availability created the desire to tell the modern generation about one of the premier explorers of our west.

Other than the author's own contributions, reference materials, including maps, come from official Federal and State sources. In addition to the original U.S. Government report, the author acknowledges use of official road maps from the states of Oregon, California, and Nevada. Also acknowledged are maps used by aviators (World Aeronautical Chart, or WAC). These have been of major importance because the details they show often do not appear on road maps. Details have been further clarified with Aviation Sectional Charts and state maps by the U.S. Geological Survey. Official highway maps for Oregon and Nevada show latitude and longitude lines but they are dim and have been emphasized. The California State road map does not show these lines -- they have been added. The current availability of the GPS (Global Positioning System) gives importance to lines of longitude and latitude so that the tourist, by car or on foot, can follow Fremont's route. Photographs are by the author.

My wife, Rita, has been invaluable with help of several kinds. She has proof-read the manuscript several times and made important suggestions. She has traveled with me in following parts of Fremont's original route and has taken some of the photographs. And she has displayed much patience in the many hours I have spent at the keyboard, scanner, and interpreting maps.

John L. Stewart

Vancouver, Washington
July, 1999

Other Books by J. L. Stewart:

The Forbidden Diary. A B-24 Navigator Remembers.
McGraw-Hill, 1998. Details of 31 missions over Nazi
Germany in 1943-44.

The following 3 textbooks used at university senior and
graduate levels in electrical engineering are long out of
print. Content is mostly applied mathematics.
  Circuit Theory and Design. John Wiley and sons, Inc.,
1956.
  Circuit Analysis of Transmission Lines. John Wiley and
sons, 1958.
  Fundamentals of Signal Theory. McGraw-Hill, 1960.

A self-published book supporting ongoing research
activities:
  The Bionic Ear. Santa Rita Technology Inc. 1979.

FOREWORD

As will be stated in the beginning of Chapter 1, only part of Fremont's complete trip, starting from and returning to Kansas, is described. In order to maximize appeal to residents of different parts of the west, and in order to limit the cost of the finished book, the presentation has been separated into two volumes. The first volume includes a brief accounting of the outbound trip from Kansas to the Dalles, followed by a detailed presentation going south from there, through Oregon and Nevada to Pyramid Lake, where he feasts on salmon trout provided by friendly Indians. The second volume, somewhat longer than the first, covers the trip from Pyramid Lake to Utah Lake, followed by a summary of the final leg back to Kansas. The original Report to the Congress includes tables of astronomical observations and travel distances. These tables, for the entire trip, are included in the Appendix to Volume 1.

The final chapter in this first volume discusses the nature of the hunter-gatherer "savages" that he encountered. Although more than half of his experiences with Indians took place after he departed from Pyramid Lake, information pertaining to these cultures is worthy of presentation in this volume. What Fremont observed is supported by earlier reports from Captains Cook and Vancouver as well as Thomas Jefferson and others. What these other observers reported can be found in an unlikely place, namely, the first half of the epic work of Thomas Malthus. Fremont probably was not aware of this source of information. Some of what Malthus presents is contained in Chapter 5.

TOPICS IN VOLUME 2

Volume 2 continues the story. It recounts Fremont's travels from the time he leaves Pyramid Lake until he returns to Kansas. All of his words are repeated until he departs from Utah Lake on the final leg of the journey.

After leaving Pyramid Lake, he "wandered" around, not knowing where he was, trying to make sense out of grossly faulty maps that were more myth than fact. He crossed the Sierra Nevada Mountains of California via the Carson Pass in the dead of winter and reached Sutter's Fort on the Sacramento River where gold was discovered four years later, setting off the remarkable California gold rush.

From there he traveled the length of California's central valley, then to the desert over what is now called the Tehachapi Pass. His travels in the desert, close to the southern rim of Death Valley, were marked by repeated encounters with Indians, a massacre of a small Mexican caravan, and the death by Indians of one of his most valuable men.

Crossing the desert through the town of Tecopa, California, he passed through what is now the city of Las Vegas and then along the Rio Virgen. He traveled through the modern city of Mesquite to Littlefield in the northwest corner of Arizona. Blocked by a chasm, he turned north to the Santa Clara River and then along the Sevier River to Utah Lake. He admired the region for its agricultural potential and his report was responsible for bringing Mormons to the area. The trip from Utah Lake back to Kansas was punctuated by threatening encounters with warring Indian tribes.

CHAPTER 1: THE OUTWARD JOURNEY

An Introduction:

In the years 1843 to 1844, Brevet Captain John C. Fremont made a momentous journey, circumnavigating much of the western part of this country and helping to set the stage for assimilation by the United States of the Northwest and California. This book recounts part of that journey. The presentation is word for word from the Report to the Congress published in 1845, with our comments and clarifications made apparent with text of reduced size and line width except for relatively long passages where our comments are designated with sub-headings.

A Brevet Captain has the rank but not the full salary of a regular army Captain. Fremont was not a West Point graduate which sometimes led to difficulties. He was educated in the traditional college way with both mathematics and classics. By education and knowledge, he was well suited for "scientific" exploration.

The original "Report to the Congress" was prepared in close cooperation with his young wife Jessie. Its readability can be credited to her. But in those days, a female could hardly be shown as the co-author of a military report!

Fremont met many Indians in his travels. He got along well with most of them, including some that may never before have seen white or black men. His comments and observations provide a unique and candid commentary, some called murderers and thieves (one of his party was killed), while others were considered to be industrious and intelligent. Many of the smaller desert tribes have long since perished. Fremont's comments augment what little is known about them.

Part of the route is shown in Figure 1.1 as a closed loop over the western part of the country. We do not recount the entire journey -- only that part with the bolder line in Figure 1.1 is included in detail. The path from Missouri to

Salt Lake and the return from Utah Lake are not shown in Figure 1.1. The small numbers on the map refer to incidents and places of some interest. These are briefly defined in the table caption for Figure 1.1, along with numbers that refer to specific chapters.

The first chapter describes the trip from Kansas where it started to the Dalles of Oregon. The dotted line covers the part from Salt Lake to the Dalles. Most of Chapter 1 is a mixture of our own comments and excerpts from the report. What we have added is meant to clarify names and places and interesting facts.

Note: Dalles is the name of a particular geological feature. A city in Oregon has been given this name as The Dalles, where the word "the" is part of the name and hence is capitalized. Fremont capitalizes only the word Dalles. The dictionary defines dalle as the rapids of a river flowing over a narrow, throughlike rock-covered bed. A dam at the city of The Dalles now covers the site deep in water.

The journey up to the Dalles has not been covered with the same detail as subsequent parts of the trip for two reasons. First, we don't want the book to be too long, which might be intimidating to some. But more importantly, the presentation might then be belittled because part of the trek followed routes established by earlier trappers, some emigrants, and by the historic adventure almost 40 years earlier by Lewis and Clark. From Chapter 3 on, a true trip of discovery is revealed. Although not the first to reach the Dalles (the start of the bold line in Figure 1.1), Fremont did create maps of considerable importance to following emigrants and he collected much useful scientific data on geology, plants, and fossils. His maps earned him the title, "Pathfinder of the West." It is said that emigrants after 1845 were likely to carry two books, the bible, and Fremont's Report to the Congress.

Subsequent to Chapter 1, Fremont's report is duplicated in all detail, leaving out no words or any other of his comments. Each chapter begins with an overview of that segment of the journey. Original and modern maps trace the route. The intent is to encourage the amateur historian to follow the route by automobile -- or by foot and mule for the rugged individual.

In all chapters following this one, Fremont's words dominate. We will nevertheless add comments here and there, with these shown with indented paragraphs and reduced line widths or as clearly separate paragraphs so that the reader will not be confused between what the present author says and what the Captain says. In presenting Fremont's writings, we do not change any words, including "strange" spellings and even possible typographical errors. We do sometimes break excessively long paragraphs into two or more paragraphs. The one long and uninterrupted script has been broken into chapters in order to give the reader places to pause.

Another modification has been made in order to limit type style to the simplest form. Instead of superscripts to indicate degrees, minutes, and seconds of latitude and longitude, slash marks are employed. For example, 120/34/20 means 120 degrees, 34 minutes, and 20 seconds. For degrees without minutes, the word degrees is used instead. The words longitude (west) and latitude (north) will generally appear in the text. For temperature, the shortened word deg. is used.

A copy of Fremont's original report, along with numerous letters, is available at libraries: "The Expeditions of John Charles Fremont," Vol. 1. Edited by Donald T. Jackson and Mary Lee Spence, Univ. Illinois Press, Chicago, 1970. This is a scholarly work of biographical nature. It does not follow the route on modern maps and has not been used in producing the present book.

An excellent biography of Fremont is "Fremont. Explorer for a Restless Nation," by Ferol Egan, Doubleday & Company, Inc., Garden City, New York. 1977. Another and earlier one is "Fremont, Pathmaker of the West," by Allan Nevins, University of Nebraska Press, Lincoln,

1992. This book was first published in 1939 with subsequent revised editions. Because his wife, Jessie, was so instrumental in helping to create the report, her biography will be of interest as well. "Jessie Benton Fremont," by Pamela Herr, Franklin Watts, New York, 1987.

Also suggested are two more books. The famous Christopher "Kit" Carson joined the troop during the first part of the adventure, and it was this association that brought him real fame. A two-volume paperback describes his exploits. "Kit Carson Days," Edwin L. Sabin, University of Nebraska Press, 1935. A three volume paperback includes articles on Alexander Gode, Jospeph Walker, Jedediah Smith, and others. "Encyclopedia of Frontier Biography," Dan L. Thrupp, University of Nebraska Press, 1991.

The proper spelling of the explorer's name has an accent mark above the letter e. This mark is rarely shown in names that honor Fremont: the city of Fremont, Fremont bridge, Fremont national forest, Fremont island, and many more. I bow to the American practice and spell the name as Fremont, pronounced like Free-mont. With the accent mark, the "e" would be pronounced as in the name "Fred."

Some details about the book:

The remainder of this introduction can be skipped if the reader is anxious to discover what Fremont said -- go a few pages beyond this to the section of this chapter, "According to Fremont." You might later return for the insights contained in the following paragraphs.

The book, in two volumes, has 11 chapters. Each chapter begins with a discussion of a particular segment of the journey. Chapters are in chronological order. Chapter 2 describes the trip to Fort Vancouver to obtain supplies for going south from the Dalles, which begins with Chapter 3. Chapter 4, to Pyramid Lake, ends Volume 1 except for a commentary in Chapter 5. The tenth chapter, in Volume 2, ending when he reaches Utah lake, contains a discussion, in Fremont's words, of the overall geography of the western and southwestern parts of this land.

Chapter 11, the final chapter in Volume 2, outlines his return to Missouri, and provides a place to make additional comments that may help to better understand the man and a few of the highlights of his career. Part of this is included in Chapter 5 of Volume 1.

The Appendix provides a place for the table of latitude and longitude values covering the entire trip as presented in the original report. Where longitudes were not given or may have been in error (for the part of the journey described here), I have estimated more nearly correct values. The Appendix also contains a table of distances from one camping place to the next, presumably based on the number of steps taken by a designated member of the party.

The Appendix for both Volumes 1 and 2 is included with Volume 1.

The original hard cover report has almost 700 pages. Much of this is in the form of appendices related to celestial observations, botany, geology, distances, and meteorological observations. The report covers two separate expeditions, one to the Rocky mountains in 1842-43, and the one of interest here in 1843-44. The text (only) covering both expeditions totals almost 290 pages. The part covering travel from the Dalles to Utah lake (the solid line in Figure 1.1) takes up 90 pages of close spaced type.

Fremont's cartographer, Charles Preuss, created three maps bound in the origin report. One of these shows the Great Salt Lake and the island (now called Fremont island) from which a map of the lake was made. The latitude of the island is almost exact (within a few hundred feet). The longitude error is 6 minutes of angle, or 0.1 degree (about 6 miles). In general, we can trust Fremont's latitude measurements (barring an occasional misprint of data). But longitudes frequently show large errors - as much as 30 statute miles. The reason for this is that pocket chronometers of the day were not well compensated for temperature nor were they ruggedized to stand jolts along the road. An error of only a few minutes of longitude could put the group in a different valley or along a different stream than the one actually traversed.

There are two pull-out maps in the report. One describes part of the Bear Valley on the way to the Great Salt Lake. It is not included. The other one goes from where Fremont entered the High Sierra region until he reaches Sutter's Fort. Its original scale is 5 miles to the inch. Only part of this map is included (in Volume 2) and it has been reduced in scale in order to fit the printed page. Neither pull-out map shows latitudes or longitudes.

It is apparent that many, if not most, celestial observations for longitude were analyzed and evaluated after Fremont's return with these values included in the report. The data were later used by Preuss to produce a single large map showing the explorations of both 1842-43 and 1843-44. This large map, which we refer to as the Preuss map, was published in 1846, one year after the report was published. Its scale is small at 1:3,000,000 (47.35 miles per inch), and it has been further compressed in order to fit the pages of the book. The route is shown with an almost invisible dashed line with small filled triangles representing camping spots. But no dates. Latitude and longitude lines are in one degree increments. (The 3 by 5 foot map is available from a contract printer via National Archives and Records Division of the U. S. Government.) We do not present a picture of the complete map. However, parts of it are reproduced along with various road, geological survey, and air maps in order to track the party during individual segments of the journey.

When Fremont was at a known location, and if he then made appropriate celestial observations, he could reset his chronometer. At least for a few days thereafter, longitude values might not be too far off. How big could errors become? At the pass over the Sierra Nevada mountains, now known as Carson pass (over a sub-range of mountains known as the Carson range), Fremont gives longitude as 120/25/57. According to modern maps, this should be slightly less than 119 degrees for an error of 26 minutes (almost 23 statute miles). The Preuss map shows this error as well. Another indication of longitude error is the value at a "large mountain lake," no doubt Lake Tahoe (which Fremont did not name). The same 26 minute error is apparent.

Fremont can be faulted for the practice of giving angles to the nearest second. This does not follow convention in the field of "theory of measurements." For longitudes, accuracy was rarely within minutes rather than seconds. He should have rounded off longitudes to the nearest minute, or at most the nearest half-minute. I rather doubt that the sextant instrument itself was precise to within a few seconds. For latitudes, tenths of minutes should be the limit. Modern marine sextants do not provide for smaller increments than tenths of a minute, which is 6 seconds of arc. This is 0.1 minute of arc which is 0.1 nautical mile of latitude and about 0.08 nautical mile of longitude at medium latitudes. The corresponding longitude error is only about 500 feet.

I have estimated correct longitude wherever possible, using a combination of latitude, terrain, and distances. My values are shown in the far right column in the Appendix next to the values given by Fremont. A table of distances walked day by day is included in Fremont's report. Part of this table also is included in the Appendix. Distance measurements are difficult to interpret because a straight line path was generally not followed and variations were not confirmed in the text. In addition, distances between points during walking were not always related to astronomical measurements or to places of encampment.

I have tried to trace Fremont's route in more detail than that revealed by Preuss. Some modern biographers have relied upon uncorrected locations. A major difficulty can be traced to our modern day cartographers. Most road maps do not show all highways, even though paved. And some show roads that are wrongly located, and few terrain features are displayed. Not all of them show latitude and longitude lines. Official State maps for Oregon and Nevada show these lines which have been darkened for easy reading here. The official California State map does not show these lines; they have been inserted for the benefit of our readers. Several maps do not show some towns, or even highways through these towns. Perhaps the most glaring example of this relates to the town of Tecopa in the desert of California which few road maps show (described in Chapter 9). Inadequacy of road maps is dramatically demonstrated in the official State of California road map. The popular tourist spot of Scotty's castle in Death Valley is not shown, nor is the highway passing through it! Some maps of states by the Department of the Interior Geological Survey fail to show all roads (partly because these maps are not always kept current). The most complete picture is often provided by (current) aviation sectional charts, although these do not differentiate between paved and unpaved roads, nor do they provide highway numbers. Aviation Sectional charts have double the resolution of the WAC charts used here. We defer further discussion of maps and charts to Chapter 2.

Details related to distance measurements: The relationships between miles, nautical miles, kilometers, and degrees of latitude and longitude can be important to the proper understanding of Fremont's route.

One degree of latitude = 60 nautical miles (nm).
One minute of latitude = one nm.
One nautical mile = 1.1508 statute miles.
One nautical mile = 1.852 kilometers.
One statute mile = 1.609 kilometers.

At the equator, one degree of longitude = 60 nm and one minute is one nautical mile. The distance represented by a change in longitude decreases towards zero as the cosine of the latitude. At 45 degrees latitude, one minute of longitude is 0.707 nautical mile.

According to Fremont:

REPORT

WASHINGTON CITY, *March* 1, 1845.

Colonel J. J. Abert,

Chief of the Corps of Topographical Engineers:

Sir: In pursuance of your instructions, to connect the reconnoissance of 1842, which I had the honor to conduct, with the surveys of Commander Wilkes on the coast of the Pacific ocean, so as to give a connected survey of the interior of our continent, I proceeded to the Great West early in the spring of 1843 and arrived, on the 17th of May, at the little town of Kansas, on the Missouri frontier, near the junction of the Kansas river with the Missouri river, where I was detained near two weeks in completing the necessary preparations for the extended explorations which my instructions contemplated.

My party consisted principally of Creole and Canadian French, and Americans, amounting in all to 39 men; among whom you will recognise several of those who were with me in my first expedition, and who have been favorably brought to your notice in a former report. Mr. Thomas Fitzpatrick, whom many years of hardship and exposure in the western territories had rendered familiar with a portion of the country it was designed to explore, had been selected as our guide; and Mr. Charles Preuss, who had been my assistant in the previous journey, was again associated with me in the same capacity on the present expedition. Agreeably to your directions, Mr. Theodore Talbot, of Washington city, had been attached to the party, with a view to advancement in his profession; and at St. Louis I had been joined by Mr. Frederick Dwight, a gentleman of Springfield, Massachusetts, who availed himself of our overland journey to visit the Sandwich islands and China, by way of Fort Vancouver.

The men engaged for the service were

Alexis Ayot	Louis Menard,
Francois Badeau,	Louis Montreuil,
Oliver Beaulieu,	Samual Neal,
Baptiste Bernier,	Alexis Pera,
John A. Campbell,	Francois Pera,
John G. Campbell,	James Power,
Manuel Chapman,	Raphael Proue,
Ransom Clark,	Oscar Sarpy,
Philibert Courteau,	Baptiste Tabeau,
Michel Crelis,	Charles Taplin,
William Creuss,	Baptiste Tesson,
Clinton Deforest,	Auguste Vasquez,
Baptiste Derosier,	Joseph Verrot,
Basil Lajeunesse,	Patrick White,
Fralleois Lajeunesse,	Tiery Wright,
Henry Lee,	Louis Zindel, and

Jacob Dodson, a free young colored man of Washington city, who volunteered to accompany the expedition, and performed his duty manfully throughout the voyage. Two Delaware Indians--a fine-looking old man and his son were engaged to accompany the expedition as hunters, through the kindness of Major Cummings, the excellent Indian agent. L. Maxwell, who had accompanied the expedition as one of the hunters in 1843, being on his way to Taos, in New Mexico, also joined us at this place.

The party was armed generally with Hall's carbines, which, with a brass 12-lb. howitzer, had been furnished to me from the United States arsenal at St. Louis, agreeably to the orders of Colonel S. W. Kearney, commanding the 3d military division. Three men were especially detailed for the management of this piece, under the charge of Louis Zindel, a native of Germany, who had been 19 years a non-commissioned officer of artillery in the Prussian army, and regularly instructed in the duties of his profession. The camp equipage and provisions were transported in twelve carts, drawn each by two mules; and a light covered wagon, mounted on good springs, had been provided for the safer carriage of the instruments.

These were:

One refracting telescope, by Frauenhofer.

One reflecting circle, by Gambey.

Two sextants, by Troughton.

One pocket chronometer, No. 837, by Goffe, Falmouth.

One pocket chronometer, No. 739, by Brockbank.

One syphon barometer, by Bunten, Paris.

One cistern barometer, by Frye & Shaw, New York.

Six thermometers, and a member of small compasses.

To make the exploration as useful as possible, I determined, in conformity to your general instructions, to vary the route to the Rocky mountains from that followed in the year 1842. The route then was up the valley of the Great Platte river to the South Pass, in north latitude 42 degrees; the route now determined on was up the valley of the Kansas river, and to the head of the Arkansas, and to some pass in the mountains, if any could be found, at the sources of that river.

By making this deviation from the former route, the problem of a new road to Oregon and California, in a climate more genial, might be solved; and a better knowledge obtained of an important river, and the country it drained, while the great object of the expedition would find its point of commencement at the termination of the former, which was at that great gate in the ridge of the Rocky mountains called the South Pass, and on to the lofty peak of the mountain which overlooks it, deemed the highest peak in the ridge, and from the opposite sides of which four great rivers take their rise, and flow to the Pacific or the Mississippi.

Various obstacles delayed our departure until the morning of the 29th, when we commenced our long voyage; and at the close of the day, rendered disagreeably cold by incessant rain, encamped about four miles beyond the frontier, on the verge of the great prairies.

Miscellaneous Comments:

Several paragraphs of our comments follow in order to clarify what has been said thus far by Fremont and also to describe some interesting observations that he made during the first part of the journey.

The date of the departure was May 29, 1843.

The Sandwich Islands later became the Hawaiian Islands.

The mountain peak cited by Fremont as the highest peak in the ridge may be the highest in that particular ridge. But it is not the highest mountain in the general Rocky Mountain area. (Some authors tend to "nit pick" on such minor errors.)

The terminus of the first part of the expedition would prove to be the Dalles of Oregon on the Columbia River. Fremont, with part of his troup, traveled on to Fort Vancouver, a trading post of the (English) Hudson Bay Company, for supplies. This post was established about 1825.

Fort Vancouver has been restored as an historic site and boasts a nice museum with frequent guided tours. It is close to downtown Vancouver, Washington, which is directly across the Columbia River from Portland, Oregon.

The cannon was acquired without direct approval from army headquarters. The policy was to not venture west in a manner that suggested an invasion because of "sensitive" matters existing with Mexican and English governments. Fremont wanted it in order to intimidate possible unfriendly Indian groups, which it apparently did. But a "disaster" almost resulted. An order was sent for Fremont to return to Washington City to explain the matter while a different officer might be sent to replace him. Hearing of this, Jessie Fremont dispatched a special letter urging him to proceed immediately so as to be beyond reach by the time that the messenger from the army arrived. Jessie was Fremont's strongest supporter with some of his same disregard for authority.

His equipment included Hall's carbines. These were relatively new at the time. They were breech loaded which permitting much faster reloading than was possible with the older style where powder, wad, and ball had to be loaded from the muzzle end. In other respects the rifle was similar to older styles with the flint-lock mechanism that would create a spark to ignite a small bit of gunpowder like a fuse. The barrel was rifled and overall length was about 53 inches. About 17,000 were manufactured between 1817 and 1840. The Army adopted this rifle in 1819. These are now prized collectors' items.

Early during the trip, Fremont crossed the path of a wagon train guided by J.B. Chiles. Wagons contained, among other things, an entire set of lumber mill machinery that Mr. Chiles planned to erect on the Sacramento river. Could this have been intended for Sutter's mill where gold was discovered in 1848?

Several men joined the expedition during travel from Kansas to the Dalles. First was Mr. William Gilpin of Missouri. In mid July, Charles Townes was added. Another man, already somewhat known as a hunter and trapper, and who would gain great fame as a result of his association with Fremont on this trip, was Christopher "Kit" Carson. We now have Carson river, Carson pass, and Carson City, the capitol of Nevada. A few days later, another hunter-trapper, Alexander Godey, joined the group. Fremont says

"In courage and professional skill he was a formidable rival of Carson."

At Upton's fort, a Frenchman had been murdered, leaving an Indian widow and two small children. This family joined the party so she could go back to her people of the Snake nation. Her children added to the liveliness of the camp.

Early in the trip, Maxwell rode into camp chased for 9 miles by Osage Indians who were ignorant of the size of Fremont's group and were chased in turn. In August, 70 mounted Indians, Arapahoes and Cheyannes, attacked but stopped when they realized that the party did not consist of their Indian enemies.

Throughout this part of the journey, as well as travels from the Dalles, Indians had constantly been at war with one another. Each group claimed land for hunting and food gathering that was fixed in area and unable to grow to support larger populations without trespassing on lands claimed by other tribes. This classic example of "turf wars" had been going on for ages and did not really end until the population was greatly reduced by diseases for which the Indians had no natural immunity. The survivors, relatively few in number, gradually acquired immunity from European diseases. This is a clear and obvious example of the process of natural selection as would be taught by Charles Darwin a generation later.

The route near Denver shows a journey southward and then a return over much the same path. The reason for this was an attempt to find an alternate path over the Rocky Mountains, which was not found.

After crossing the Rocky Mountains, Fremont identified the embryonic Colorado river and a major tributary, the Green river. He was tempted to go south to verify reports of almost mystical nature concerning huge chasms and vertical walls associated with the river. What was being described was the Grand Canyon, which was then an essentially unknown region (except to a few Indians).

The last part of August saw Fremont deviating from the initial plan in order to explore the Great Salt Lake. This hundred mile "side trip" was to an area still cloaked in mystery. The lake had no visible outlet with stories about a whirlpool in its center that guided water to the sea. The area was mapped for the first time. Figure 1.2 is contained in the report to the Congress. Fremont, Carson, and others used a rubber boat to go to an island in the lake. (It is not known if the rubber had been vulcanized. Goodyear invented the process only a few years before, in 1839.) They were probably the first humans to set foot there and they climbed to the highest point on the place where they could survey and map the area. They saw mostly salt marshes and salt beds that did not appear promising for agriculture. Fremont named the island Disappointment Island for this reason. Later, on his return trip, he visited Utah Lake and then realized that the area was good for agriculture. The island is now called Fremont Island and his maps and descriptions are credited with bringing the Mormons, under the leadership of Brigham Young, to the area.

Maps intended for use by emigrants were completed by Mr. Preuss in 1846. These are different from the large map described earlier. They do not show details of the side trip to Salt Lake. With a scale of 10 miles to the inch, they show the direct overland route from the point where the Kansas river meets the Missouri river to the point where the Walla Walla river enters the Columbia river. We do not present or discuss these maps because the part of the trip of primary interest to us is not presented. (Note: Fremont defines the river with the Indian name, Walahwalah.)

When Fremont was on the trip to Salt Lake, he comments on the decline of the buffalo. They began to diminish rapidly about 1834 with large areas becoming practically empty of them in only a few years. Killing for meat and hides for robes and skins for Indian lodges (new every year) is blamed for the decline. Shortages in an area where Indians depended on buffalo for existence resulted in wars of extermination between tribes living in areas having different numbers of buffalo. The warfare did not last -- it ended when virtually all buffalo were exterminated. Fremont shows great concern for this situation with several pages in the report. Clearly, he was a conservationist concerned with maintaining a constant wildlife population.

After the side trip to Salt Lake, the group reached Fort Hall on the Snake river. This river was also referred to as the Lewis Fork of the Columbia River. Today, the only name is Snake river. Indians in the area were poor but happy, feasting on salmon or hungry and almost naked for lack of animal skins. Figure 1.3 from the report shows the American Falls of the Lewis Fork.

The next resting place was Fort Boise, a Hudson Bay trading post, near present day Boise, Idaho. The Fort's manager, Mr. Payette, described local Indians in terms of feast or famine. A paragraph from the report is worth repeating here:

According to Fremont:

Pointing to a group of Indians who had just arrived from the mountains on the left side of the valley, and who were regarding our usual appliances of civilization with an air of bewildered curiosity, Mr. Payette informed me that, ever since his arrival at this post, he had unsuccessfully endeavored to induce these people to lay up a store of salmon for their winter provision. While the summer weather and salmon lasted, they lived contentedly and happily, scattered along the different streams where the fish were to be found; and as soon as winter snows began to fall, little smokes would be seen rising among the mountains, where they would be found in miserable groups, starving out the winter; and sometimes, according to the general belief, reduced to the horror of cannibalism - the strong, of course, preying on the weak. Certain it is, they are driven to any extremity for food, and eat every insect, and every creeping thing, however loathsome and repulsive. Snails, lizards, ants - all are devoured with the readiness and greediness of mere animals.

Miscellaneous Comments:

Indeed, some Indian tribes showed a credible level of sophistication and social organization. But there were some, existing in peripheral regions, that displayed a stone age mentality with little evidence of social or cultural planning.

In the region of the Blue mountains, Fremont remarks that pines were 3 to 7 feet in diameter and 200 feet high. Some of the white spruces measured 12 feet in circumference and 200 feet high. These figures describe what we now call low altitude "old growth."

The party finally saw Mount Hood. Figure 1.4 shows how this might have looked to them later in the journey, looking up the Columbia River from Fort Vancouver. (See Chapter 2.) The next day they came to the missionary establishment of Dr. Whitman who was not present, being on a trip to Fort Vancouver. At that time, the place boasted only one adobe hut. There was a fine looking and large family of emigrants. A small village of Nez Percé Indians ("Pierced Nose") was nearby.

Three years after Femont's visit, Indians of the Cayuse tribe massacred people at the mission, including Dr. Whitman, his wife, and eleven white emigrants. The reason for their ire was partly because Dr. Whitman's interests had turned from helping the Indians to helping emigrants. A second reason was that measles, brought in by emigrants, was sickening and killing few emigrants while devastating the Indian settlement. The Indians may have believed that their high death rate involved a conspiracy or witchcraft. The Whitmans' insensitivity to the cultural habits and history of the Indians certainly did not help. The Whitman Mission is now a National Historic Site. This massacre gave an excuse to claim the Oregon territory for the United States. A forest in northeastern Oregon is now called the Wallowa Whitman National Forest.

The next day of travel brought the party to view the impressive expanse of the Columbia river. The party then went down the river by rubber boat to within a few miles of the John Day river where they changed to land travel. They forded this river and later the Fall river, also referred to as Riviere aux Chutes. Today it is called the Dechutes river.

Towards the end of the trip to the Dalles, the group came upon some friendly Indians and then into a pretty valley populated by a less admirable group. Fremont says:

According to Fremont:

In comparison with the Indians of the Rocky mountains and the great eastern plain, these are disagreeably dirty in their habits. Their huts were crowded with half-naked women and children, and the atmosphere within any thing but pleasant to persons who had just been riding in the fresh morning air. We were somewhat amused with the scanty dress of one women, who, in common with the others, rushed out of the huts on our arrival, and who, in default of other covering, used a child as a fig leaf.

The road in about half an hour passed near an elevated point, from which we overlooked the valley of the Columbia for many miles, and saw in the distance several houses surrounded by fields, which a chief, who had accompanied us from the village, pointed out to us as the Methodist missionary station.

In a few miles we descended to the river, which we reached at one of its remarkably interesting features, known as the *Dalles of the Columbia.* The whole volume of the river at this place passed between the walls of a chasm, which has the appearance of having been rent through the basaltic strata which form the valley rock of the region. At the narrowest place we found the breadth, by measurement,

58 yards, and the average height of the walls above the water 25 feet; forming a trough between the rocks - whence the name, probably applied by a Canadian voyageur. The mass of waters, in the present low state of the river, passed swiftly between, deep and black, and curled into many small whirlpools and counter currents, but unbroken by foam, and so still that scarcely the sound of a ripple was heard. The rock, for a considerable distance from the river, was worn over a large portion of its surface into circular holes and well-like cavities, by the abrasion of the river, which, at the season of high waters, is spread out over the adjoining bottoms.

In the recent passage through this chasm, an unfortunate event had occurred to Mr. Applegate's party, in the loss of one of their boats, which had been carried under water in the midst of the *Dalles,* and two of Mr. Applegate's children and one man drowned. This misfortune was attributed only to want of skill in the steersman, as at this season there is no impediment to navigation; although the place is entirely impassable at high water when boats pass safely over the great falls above, in the submerged state in which they then find themselves.

The basalt here is precisely the same as that which constitutes the rock of the valley higher up the Columbia, being very compact, with a few round cavities.

We passed rapidly three or four miles down the level valley, and encamped near the mission. The character of the forest growth here changed, and we found ourselves, with pleasure, again among oaks and other forest trees of the east, to which we had long been strangers; and the hospitable and kind reception with which we were welcomed among our country people at the mission aided the momentary illusion of home.

Two good-looking wooden dwelling houses, and a large school house, with stables, barn, and garden, and large cleared fields between the houses and the river bank, on which were scattered the wooden huts of an Indian village, gave to the valley the cheerful and busy air of civilization, and had in our eyes an appearance of abundant and enviable comfort.

Miscellaneous Comments:

Jessie Applegate was part of a covered wagon train in 1843, arriving at the Columbia River only a short time before Fremont's party. Although he had no official position at the outset, he came to be an honored and respected member of the party. He traveled with two of his brothers. One child each of these brothers was drowned along with the 70 year old uncle. With grief as the motivator, Jessie Applegate later sought to find a better way to the Willamette valley. In 1846 he brought a wagon train over the Nevada desert, following some trails previously traveled by Fremont (as described in Volume 2). Following the much-used overland trail, he deviated near the town of Imlay, Nevada and headed northwest, then across the mountains into southern Oregon and up to the Willamette valley to finally settle in the area of what is now Salem, the Capital of Oregon. The trail that he defined came to be known as the Applegate trail.

The wagon train with the Applegates started from Kansas about the same time as Fremont began his trip. There were almost a thousand people and a 120 wagons in the group. It included Mr. Chiles, the Applegates, and Dr. Whitman. The paths of the wagons and Fremont's party frequently came together. The wagons went direct towards their destination. Fremont made two major "side trips," one in search of an alternative to the South Pass through the Rocky Mountains (to no avail), and another to explore the Great Salt Lake. Because his group could travel faster than the wagon train, he was able to catch up with them. When Fremont comments on emigrants and wagons waiting for means to travel down the Columbia River, he is referring to this particular wagon train. It is important to history to realize that this was the first emigrant train that was able to go all the way to Oregon with wagons. Indeed, other adventurers and emigrants had previously followed the trail, but none was able to get wagons much beyond Fort Hall.

An account of this history making wagon train, including quotes from Fremont, is "Blazing a Wagon Train to Oregon," by Lloyd W. Coffman. Echo Books, Springfield, Oregon, 1993.

Both Fremont and the wagon train reached the Methodist Missionary near the Dalles. An organized group of Methodists established several missions in the northwest during the 1830s. The first missionary at the Dalles was Jason Lee. He and others would preach to large groups of Gorge Indians from a small rock, perhaps 15 feet high. The "Pulpit Rock" is shown in Figure 1.5. It is located on a special island in the middle of 12-th street in the city of The Dalles. Mr. Perkins was the resident missionary when Fremont was there.

Here we end our description of the first part of Fremont's expedition. Time at the Dalles was used to prepare for travel in a southerly direction into areas that remained unexplored and not traveled by other than Indians and a few hardy hunters and trappers. But first, a trip to Fort Vancouver, further down the Columbia River, was necessary in order to obtain supplies for the homeward journey.

Points of interest referenced to Figure 1.1

The route followed by John C. Fremont in 1843 and 1844 is shown with dotted and dashed lines. Latitudes and longitudes are in 5 degree increments. The solid line includes dates from November 5, 1843 to May 27, 1844. Circled numbers refer to events referenced to individual chapters.

Reference	Chapter	Event
1	1	Mapping the Great Salt Lake
2	1	Whitman Missionary Station
3	2	The Methodist Mission at the Dalles
4	2	Fort Vancouver
5	3	Great Basin seen from Winter Ridge
6	4	Christmas at Christmas Lake
7	4	New Year's Day
8	4	Pyramid Lake
9	6	Near modern town of Bridgeport
10	6	At Carson Pass
11	7	Sutter's Fort (Nueva Helvetia)
12	8	Tehachapi Pass
13	9	North slope, San Gabriel Mountains
14	9	Reaching the Old Spanish Trail
15	9	Massacre at Hernandez Spring
16	9	Near present down town Las Vegas
17	10	The Gorge
18	10	Fremont Wash
19	10	Utah Lake
20	11	Summary of Homeward Trip

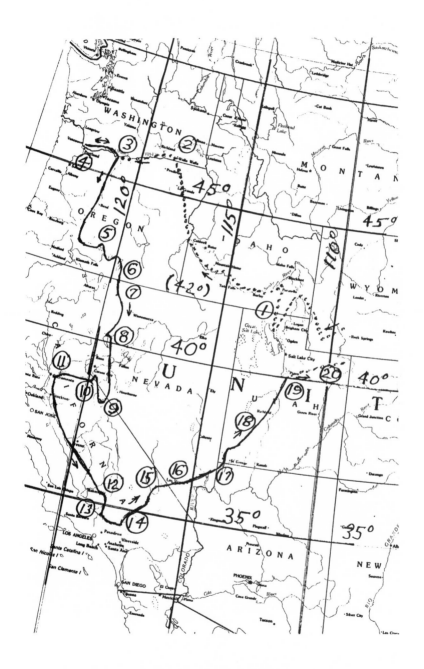

Figure 1.1. Map of the Route.

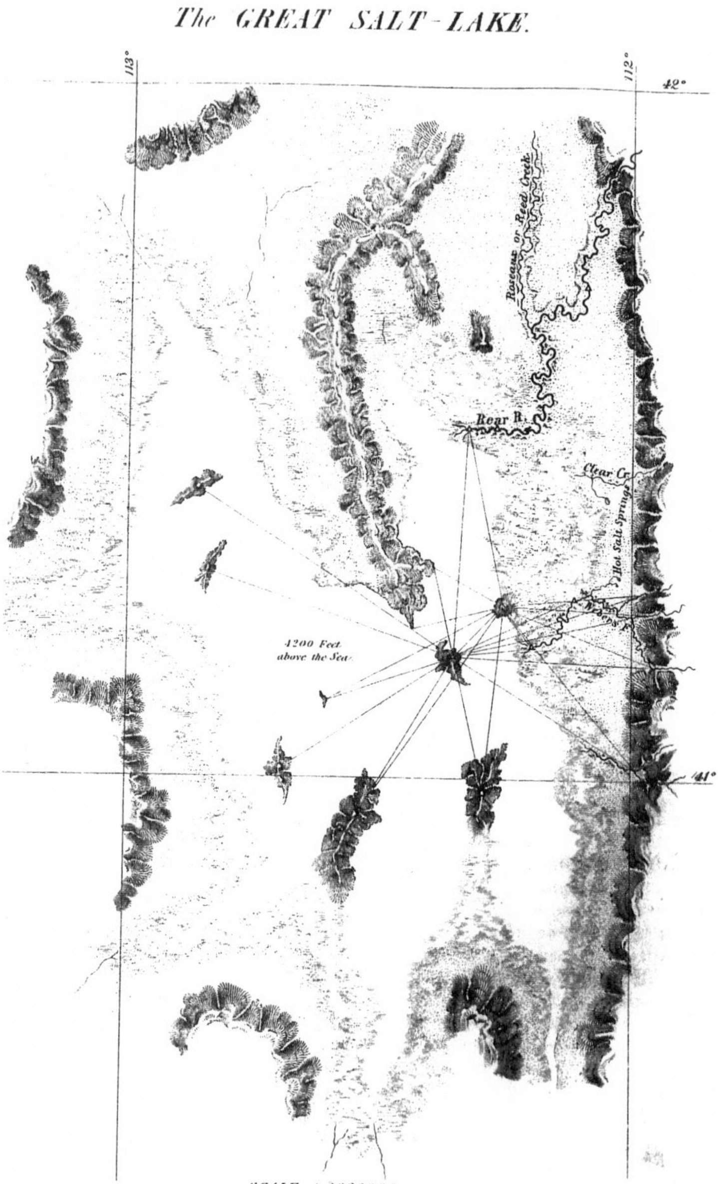

Figure 1.2. The Great Salt Lake. From the Report.

THE AMERICAN FALLS OF LEWIS FORK.

Figure 1.3. The American Falls. From the Report

Figure 1.4. Mt. Hood as seen from near Fort Vancouver.

Figure 1.5. Pulpit Rock in The Dalles.

CHAPTER 2: TO FORT VANCOUVER

Introduction:

On November 5, the Fremont party reached the Methodist missionary station at the Dalles of the Columbia River. Fremont, with three other members of the party, along with Indians to manage water travel, proceeded down the Columbia to Fort Vancouver. When loaded with supplies, they returned to join up with the main party that had remained at the Dalles to collect horses and other animals in preparation for the long and circuitous journey home. Much of the return trip from the Dalles turned out to be unplanned. This was actually fortunate because of the wealth of additional geographical data that were accumulated. The unplanned route also provided valuable information about the cultures of the Indian tribes that were met along the way.

Fremont does not give a day by day accounting for the time he left the Dalles until he reached Fort Vancouver on November 8. He left Fort Vancouver on November 10th, arriving back at the missionary station on November 18. No latitudes or longitudes are logged except for one value on November 11, which does not appear to provide useful information. The party would remain at the missionary station until November 25.

Figures 2.1-a, b, and c are from the 1846 Preuss map. In order to fit the pages of the book, the map has been segmented into three parts that add with decreasing latitude. In all cases, true north is upward when the figure is oriented for letter reading. Figure 2.1-a shows the route along the Columbia River from near Fort Walahwalah to Fort Vancouver. In b, the route south from the Dalles extends through Summer Lake as described in Chapter 3. Figure 2.1-c extends further south to include Pyramid Lake as described in Chapter 4. Marks near map segment boundaries are meant to clarify the places where the different segments join.

Circles on this and following maps locate Fremont's route. The larger circles correspond to places where astronomical observations were made. The smaller circles are the author's estimates. Locations designated with large circles have been adjusted to correct for Fremont's lognitude errors on maps for Figures 2.2 and 2.3. (With circles to designate the route, map details are less covered than when a heavy line is used.)

Figure 2.2-a, b, c, d, and e is in six parts (on 5 pages). In general it follows the Preuss map. The first 4 parts come from the official road map for the State of Oregon. The last two parts, at a different scale, come from the official road map for the State of Nevada. The latitude and longitude lines on these road maps have been darkened; in the natural state they are difficult to see.

Figures 2.3 in 6 segments comes from an aviation World Aeronautical Chart (WAC), a publication of the U.S. Government. This map shows much the same region as the road map of Figures 2.2. Latitude and longitude lines are clearly defined on WAC charts along with considerable terrain detail and roads, both paved and unpaved (but detail is not as complete as on aeronautical Sectional Charts). Superimposed aeronautical symbols should be ignored except, perhaps, for those following the route by airplane or helicopter.

Comparing modern maps to the Preuss map reveals longitude errors. Preuss shows the Fall river emptying into the Columbia at longitude 120/34 (ignoring seconds). The air map shows this at longitude 120/54. The 20 minute difference equates to nearly 16 statute miles. The Preuss chart shows Fort Vancouver at longitude 120/40. If the old Fort Vancouver is assumed to be located at present Pearson Air Field, it is at longitude 122/37. This is not too far off, allowing for uncertainty in measuring from the small scale of the Preuss map. The table of longitudes and latitudes in the report (see Appendix) does not include values for Fort Vancouver. Perhaps Preuss used a value provided by the Hudson Bay company. Fremont did not make astronomical observations at Fort Vancouver and so could not correct his watch. The erroneous value of longitude at the mission is based on astronomical data acquired by Fremont without the benefit of a well known reference point. This error continued to affect values after leaving the Dalles on the southward segment of the journey.

We should perhaps forgive Fremont for not correcting his watch through observations at a known location. Citizens in this part of the Northwest are all too familiar with long periods during winter when the sky is rarely seen.

According to Fremont:

Our land journey found here its western termination. The delay involved in getting our camp to the right bank of the Columbia, and in opening a road through the continuous forest to Vancouver, rendered a journey along the river impracticable; and on this side the usual road across the mountain required strong and fresh animals, there being an interval of three days in which they could obtain no food. I therefore wrote immediately to Mr. Fitzpatrick, directing him to abandon the carts at the Walahwalah missionary station, and, as soon as the necessary pack saddles could be made, which his party required, meet me at the Dalles, from which point I proposed to commence our homeward journey.

> By "right bank," Fremont appears to refer to the side looking upstream. This means that he was located on the south side of the river in what is now the State of Oregon. Walahwalah is on the north side of the Columbia in what is now the state of Washington. However, it is possible that this definition may not have been followed consistently.

The day after our arrival being Sunday, no business could be done at the mission; but on Monday Mr. Perkins assisted me in procuring from the Indians a large canoe, in which I designed to complete our journey to Vancouver, where I expected to obtain the necessary supply of provisions and stores for our winter journey. Three Indians, from the family to whom the canoe belonged, were engaged to assist in working her during the voyage, and, with them, our water party consisted of Mr. Preuss and myself, with Bernier and Jacob Dodson. In charge of the party which was to remain at the Dalles I left Carson, with instructions to occupy the people in making pack saddles and refitting their equipage.

The village from which we were to take the canoe was on the right bank of the river, about ten miles below, at the mouth of the Tinanens creek; and while Mr. Preuss proceeded down the river with the instruments, in a little canoe paddled by two Indians, Mr. Perkins accompanied me with the remainder of the party by land. The last of the emigrants had just left the Dalles at the time of our arrival, travelling some by water and others by land, making ark-like rafts, on which they had embarked their families and household, with their large wagons and other furniture, while their stock were driven along the shore.

For about five miles below the Dalles, the river is narrow, and probably very deep; but during this distance it is somewhat open, with grassy bottoms on the left. Entering, then, among the lower mountains of the Cascade range, it assumes a general character, and high and steep rocky hills shut it in on either side, rising abruptly in places to the height of 1,500 feet above the water, and gradually acquiring a more mountainous character as the river approaches the Cascades.

Modern maps do not show Tinanens creek. Fremont later refers to this creek as he guides his party southward from The Dalles. The discussion again indicates that right and left refer to sides when looking upstream. A long stretch of the Columbia river where steep bluffs border it on both sides has been declared a National Scenic Area. Land development and commercialization within the area are restricted.

After an hour's travel, when the sun was nearly down, we searched along the shore for a pleasant place, and halted to prepare supper. We had been well supplied by our friends at the mission with delicious salted salmon, which had been taken at the fattest season; also, with potatoes, bread, coffee, and sugar. We were delighted at a change in our mode of travelling and living. The canoe sailed smoothly down the river; at night we encamped upon the shore, and a plentiful supply of comfortable provisions supplied the first of wants. We enjoyed the contrast which it presented to our late toilsome marchings, our night watchings, and our frequent privation of food. We were a motley group, but all happy: three unknown Indians; Jacob, a colored man; Mr. Preuss, a German; Bernier, creole French; and myself.

Being now upon the ground explored by the South Sea expedition under Captain Wilkes, and having accomplished the object of uniting my survey with his, and thus presenting a connected exploration from the Mississippi to the Pacific, and the winter being at hand, I deemed it necessary to economize time by voyaging in the night, as is customary here, to avoid the high winds, which rise with the morning, and decline with the day.

In 1842, Captain Charles Wilkes, an American naval officer and explorer, completed his momentous sea journey of exploration. It included the antarctic coastal areas now known as Wilkes Land, the Hawaiian Islands, the South Pacific and Australia, the Northwest coast of the United States, and islands of Oceania. He was first to map the entrance to the Columbia river which Fremont joins with his own maps. And he is credited with the discovery of the antarctic continent. The principal purpose of Fremont's journey was to show how an overland route could match with what Wilkes had revealed.

Accordingly, after an hour's halt, we again embarked, and resumed our pleasant voyage down the river. The wind rose to a gale after several hours; but the moon was very bright, and the wind was fair, and the canoe glanced rapidly down the stream, the waves breaking into foam alongside; and our night voyage, as the wind bore us rapidly along between the dark mountains, was wild and interesting. About midnight we put to the shore on a rocky beach, behind which was a dark-looking pine forest. We built up large fires among the rocks, which were in large masses round about; and, arranging our blankets on the most sheltered places we could find, passed a delightful night.

After an early breakfast, at daylight we resumed our journey, the weather being clear and beautiful, and the river smooth and still. On either side the mountains are all pine-timbered, rocky, and high. We were now approaching one of the marked features of the lower Columbia where the river forms a great *cascade*, with a series of rapids, in breaking through the range of mountains to which the lofty peaks of Mount Hood and St. Helens belong, and which rise as great pillars of snow on either side of the passage. The main branch of the *Sacramento* river, and the *Tlamath*, issue in cascades from this range; and the Columbia, breaking through it in a succession of cascades, gives the idea of cascades to the whole range; and hence the name of the CASCADE RANGE, which it bears, and distinguishes it from the Coast Range lower down.

Fremont's presentation follows the ideas that members of the party had as they traveled along. Although the Tlamath river (the modern name is Klamath river) can be considered to issue from the Cascades, the Sacramento river can not so easily be categorized (unless the region south and southeast of Mount Shasta in Northern California can be so designated). Fremont corrects earlier concepts and beliefs in a fairly in-depth discussion upon reaching Utah lake on his return trip.

In making a short turn to the south, the river forms the cascades in breaking over a point of agglomerated masses of rock, leaving a handsome bay to the right, with several rocky pine-covered islands, and the mountains sweep at a distance around a cove where several small streams enter the bay. In less than an hour we halted on the left bank about five minutes' walk above the cascades, where there were several Indian huts, and where our guides signified it was customary to hire Indians to assist in making the portage. When travelling with a boat as light as a canoe, which may easily he carried on the shoulders of the Indians, this is much the better side of the river for the portage, as the ground here is very good and level, being a handsome bottom, which I remarked was covered (*as was now always the case along the river*) with a growth of green and fresh-looking grass.

It was long before we could come to an understanding with the Indians; but at length, when they had first received the price of their assistance in goods, they went vigorously to work; and, in a shorter time than had been occupied in making our arrangements, the canoe, instruments. and baggage, were carried through (a distance of about half a mile) to the bank below the main cascade, where we again embarked, the water being white with foam among ugly rocks, and boiling into a thousand whirlpools.

The boat passed with great rapidity, crossing and recrossing in the eddies of the current. After passing through about 2 miles of broken water, we ran some wild-looking rapids, which are called the Lower Rapids, being the last on the river, which below is tranquil and smooth - a broad, magnificent stream. On a low broad point on the right bank of the river, at the lower end of these rapids, were pitched many tents of the emigrants, who were waiting here for their friends from above, or for boats and provisions which were expected from Vancouver. In our passage down the rapids, I had noticed their camps along the shore, or transporting their goods across the portage. This portage makes a head of navigation, ascending the river. It is about two miles in length; and above, to the Dalles, is 45 miles of smooth and good navigation.

We glided on without further interruption between very rocky and high steep mountains, which sweep along the river valley at a little distance, covered with forests of pine, and showing occasionally lofty escarpments of red rock. Nearer, the shore is bordered by steep escarped hills and huge vertical rocks, from which the waters of the mountain reach the river in a variety of beautiful falls, sometimes several hundred feet in height. Occasionally along the river occurred pretty bottoms, covered with the greenest verdure of the spring. To a professional farmer, however, it does not offer many places of sufficient extent to be valuable for agriculture; and after passing a few miles below the Dalles, I had scarcely seen a place on the south shore where wagons could get to the river.

The beauty of the scenery was heightened by the continuance of very delightful weather resembling the Indian summer of the Atlantic. A few miles below the cascades we passed a singular isolated hill; and in the course of the next six miles occurred five very pretty falls from the heights on the left bank, one of them being of a very picturesque character; and towards sunset we reached a remarkable point of rocks, distinguished, on account of prevailing high winds, and the delay it frequently occasions to the canoe navigation, by the name of *Cape Horn*. It borders the river in a high wall of rock, which comes boldly down into deep water; and in violent gales down the river, and from the opposite shore, which is the prevailing direction of strong winds, the water is dashed against it with considerable violence. It appears to form a serious obstacle to canoe travelling; and I was informed by Mr. Perkins, that in a voyage up the river he had been detained two weeks at this place, and was finally obliged to return to Vancouver.

Fremont did not give names to the various waterfalls that he saw. Perhaps the most impressive of these is Multnoma Falls on the southern side of the river in Oregon. It has become a popular tourist attraction and is a state park. Figure 2.4 is a photograph of the falls. The singular isolated hill that Fremont mentions might be what is now known as Beacon Rock which also is a state park. Figure 2.5 shows this rock. Cape Horn still bears this name and is a well known viewpoint on the highway that runs along the Washington side of the river. Figure 2.6 shows this feature looking up from the shore of the river.

The winds of this region deserve a particular study. They blow in currents, which show there to be governed by fixed laws; and it is a problem how far they may come from the mountains, or from the ocean through the breaks in the mountains which let out the river.

The wind Fremont speaks of has not abated. It is called the "East Wind." Where the river is wide, these winds have brought large numbers of wind surfers to the region, especially somewhat west of the city of Hood River.

The hills here had lost something of their rocky appearance, and had already begun to decline. As the sun went down, we searched along the river for an inviting spot; and, finding a clean rocky beach, where some large dry trees were lying on the ground, we ran our boat to the shore; and, after another comfortable supper, ploughed our way along the river in darkness. Heavy clouds covered the sky this evening, and the wind began to sweep in gusts among the trees, as if bad weather were coming. As we advanced, the hills on both sides grew constantly lower; on the right, retreating from the shore, and forming a somewhat extensive bottom of intermingled prairie and wooded land.

In the course of a few hours, and opposite to a small stream coming in from the north, called the *Tea Prairie* river, the highlands on the left declined to the plains, and three or four miles below disappeared entirely on both sides, and the river entered the low country. The river had gradually expanded; and when we emerged from the highlands, the opposite shores were so distant as to appear indistinct in the uncertainty of the light.

> The name Tea Prairie river is not shown on modern maps. It is possible that the present name is Washougal river.

About 10 o'clock our pilots halted, apparently to confer about the course; and, after a little hesitation, pulled directly across an open expansion of the river, where the waves were somewhat rough for a canoe, the wind blowing very fresh. Much to our surprise, a few minutes afterwards we ran aground. Backing off our boat, we made repeated trials at various places to cross what appeared to be a point of shifting sand bars, where we had attempted to shorten the way by a cut-off. Finally, one of our Indians got into the water, and waded about until he found a channel sufficiently deep, through which we wound along after him, and in a few minutes again entered the deep water below.

As we paddled rapidly down the river, we heard the noise of a saw mill at work on the right bank; and, letting our boat float quietly down, we listened with pleasure to the unusual sounds; and before midnight encamped on the bank of the river, about a mile above Fort Vancouver. Our fine dry Weather had given place to a dark cloudy night. At midnight it began to rain, and we found ourselves suddenly in the gloomy and humid season, which in the narrow region lying between the Pacific and the Cascade mountains, and for a considerable distance along the coast, supplies the place of winter.

The location of the saw mill is now within the city limits of Vancouver, Washington. The water resource of the place now supplies a fish hatchery (Department of Fish and Wildlife). The stream does not appear on any of the maps I have used. A smaller nearby stream was the location of a grist mill (for grinding grain). Preuss shows the locations of these two mills in small letters. A sign near the location of the saw mill, on Washington State Highway 14, was erected by the Historical Sites and Markers Commission, State Highway Commission (of Washington). For some reason, this sign has recently been removed (late 1998 or early 1999). It read:

FIRST SAWMILL

A short distance south of this site on Love Creek near its confluence with the Columbia River, Hudson's Bay company employees built the first sawmill in the old Oregon country in 1827. Machinery imported from England, by sailing vessel, was powered by a water wheel. Logs were hauled from nearby forests by ox teams. The workman were French Canadians and Kanakas from the Sandwich Islands. Much of the lumber was used at Fort Vancouver, but later many shiploads were sold abroad.

In the morning, the first object that attracted my attention was the barque Columbia, lying at anchor near the landing. She was about to start on her voyage to England, and was now ready for sea; being detained only in waiting the arrival of the express batteaus, which descend the Columbia and its north fork with the overland mail from Canada and Hudson's bays which had been delayed beyond their usual time.

I immediately waited upon Dr. McLaughlin, the executive officer of the Hudson Bay Company in the territory west of the Rocky mountains who received me with the courtesy and hospitality for which he has been eminently distinguished, and which makes a forcible and delightful impression on a traveller from the long wilderness from which we had issued. I was immediately supplied by him with the necessary stores and provisions to refit and support my party in our contemplated winter journey to the States; and also with a Mackinaw boat and canoes, manned with Canadian and Iroquois voyageurs and Indians, for their transportation to the Dalles of the Columbia. In addition to this efficient kindness in funishing me with these necessary supplies, I received from him a warm and gratifying sympathy in the suffering which his great experience led him to anticipate for us in our homeward journey, and a letter of recommendation and credit for any others of the Hudson Bay Company into whose posts we might be driven by unexpected misfortune.

Of course, the future supplies for my party were paid for, bills on the Government of the United States being readily taken; but every hospitable attention was extended to me, and I accepted an invitation to take a room in the fort, *"and to make myself at home while I staid."*

I found many American emigrants at the fort; others had already crossed the river into their land of promise the Walahmette valley. Others were daily arriving; and all of them had been furnished with shelter, so far as it could be afforded by the buildings connected with the establishment. Necessary clothing and provisions (the latter to be afterwards returned in kind from the produce of their labor) were also furnished. This friendly assistance was of very great value to the emigrants, whose families were otherwise exposed to much suffering in the winter rains, which had now commenced, at the same time that they were in want of all the common necessaries of life. Those who had taken a water conveyance at the Nez Percé fort continued to arrive safely, with no other accident than has been already mentioned. The party which had passed over the Cascade mountains were reported to have lost a number of their animals; and those who had driven their stock down the Columbia had brought them safely in, and found for them a ready and very profitable market, and were already proposing to return to the States in the spring for another supply.

> The modern spelling of the Indian word Walahmette is Willamette. The "a" is pronounced as in "at" or "and," and is stressed. The final "mette" becomes a short "met."
>
> Fort Vancouver was established by the English Hudson Bay company in 1825 to serve a large part of the Pacific Northwest. It is now a National Historic Site; the fort has been restored and regular tours are offered by on-site personnel. After 1846, the fort continued operation as a British company, but actually on American soil. This continued until the company moved out in 1860. Figure 2.7 shows part of the restructured fort as it appears today.
>
> John McLaughlin trained as a physician near Montreal and joined the Hudson Bay company as a physician. He became head of the Columbia Department. He was supposed to sqeeze Americans out of the market and firmly establish the British claim to all of Oregon. He was a good businessman but also very hospitable and generous to the growing number of American settlers. When the new boundaries were declared in 1846, and with pressure from his British critics, he retired, moved to Oregon City, and became an American citizen. To Oregonians, he has become the "Father of Oregon."

In the space of two days our preparations had been completed, and we were ready to set out on our return. It would have been very gratifying to have gone down to the Pacific, and, solely in the interest and in the love of geography, to have seen the ocean on the western as well as on the eastern side of the continent, so as to give a satisfactory completeness to the geographical picture which had been formed in our minds; but the rainy season had now regularly set in, and the air was filled with fogs and rain, which left no beauty in any scenery, and obstructed observations. The object of my instructions had been entirely fulfilled in having connected our reconnoissance with the surveys of Captain Wilkes; and although it would have been agreeable and satisfactory to terminate here also our ruder astronomical observations, I was not, for such a reason, justified to make a delay in waiting for favorable weather.

Near sunset of the 10th the boats left the fort, and encamped after making only a few miles. Our flotilla consisted of a Mackinaw barge and three canoes - one of them that in which we had descended the river; and a party in all of 20 men. One of the emigrants, Mr. Burnet, of Missouri, who had left his family and property at the Dalles, availed himself of the opportunity afforded by the return of our boats to bring them down to Vancouver. This gentleman, as well as the Messrs. Applegate, and others of the emigrants whom I saw, possessed intelligence and character, with the moral and intellectual stamina, as well as the enterprise, which give solidity and respectability to the foundation of colonies.

November 11. - The morning was rainy and misty. We did not move with the practised celerity of my own camp; and it was near 9 o'clock when our motley crew had finished their breakfast and were ready to start. Once afloat, however, they worked steadily and well, and we advanced at a good rate up the river; and in the afternoon a breeze sprung up, which enabled us to add a sail to the oars. At evening we encamped on a warm-looking beach, on the right bank, at the foot of the high river hill, immediately at the lower end of Cape Horn. On the opposite shore is said to be a singular hole in the mountain, from which the Indians believe comes the wind producing these gales. It is called The Devil's Hole; and the Indians, I was told, have been resolving to send down one of their slaves to explore the region below.

We do not normally think of Indians as having slaves. These were probably prisoners of war. Apparently the Indians were great procrastinators, having never really mounted a seemingly easy exploration.

At dark, the wind shifted into its stormy quarter, gradually increasing to a gale from the southwest; and the sky becoming clear, I obtained a good observation of an emersion of the first satellite; the result of which, being an absolute observation, I have adopted for the longitude of the place.

With the aid of a relatively powerful refracting telescope, the larger moons (satellites) of Jupiter could be seen. As a selected one of these comes from behind the planet, the moment it first becomes visible marks a moment in time. Everywhere on earth where Jupiter can be viewed the emersion (i.e., emergence) of this moon comes at the same moment (within a small fraction of a second). This phenomenon serves as a clock that gives the same time as a clock at a distant observatory. Knowing the time, a local clock can be set. Then with a second observation of a star, a line of position (LOP) can be obtained. A separate observation to find latitude, perhaps using polaris, can be represented as an east-west line. If the LOP crosses this line at a not-too-small angle, a fix is obtained to then give longitude. An alternative to a value for latitude is a second LOP that crosses the first one at a not-too-small angle.

An emersion (or immersion when the satellite disappears behind the planet) is not easy to pinpoint in time, and thus accuracy is limited. The method is not mentioned in current books on navigation. Fremont probably did not do the calculations to find location by this method because tables of emersion and immersion would have to be long and complex. But if similar measurements were made at an observatory, locations could be determined and/or verified when Fremont returned to civilization by comparing what his chronometer showed when the observation was made with what it should have been.

During the 1700's and into the 1800's, large prizes were offered to the person who could show how to accurately determine longitude at sea. The competition seemed to be between making an accurate clock and fully developing the immersion/emersion concept along with certain measurements involving occultation of the moon. The clock approach, developed by John Harrison in England, ultimately won the prize. The interested reader is directed to "Longitude. The Story of a Lone Genius Who Solved the Greatest Scientific Problem of His Time," Dava Sobel, Penguin Books, New York, NY, 1995.

November 12. - The wind during the night had increased to so much violence that the broad river this morning was angry and white; the waves breaking with considerable force against this rocky wall of the cape. Our old Iroquois pilot was unwilling to risk the boats around the point, and I was not disposed to hazard the stores of our voyage for the delay of a day. Further observations were obtained during the day, giving for the latitude of the place 45/33/09; and the longitude, obtained from the satellite, is 122/6/15.

November 13. - We had a day of disagreeable and cold rain; and, late in the afternoon, began to approach the rapids of the cascades. There is here a high timbered island on the left shore, below which, in descending, I had remarked in a bluff on the river the extremities of trunks of trees appearing to be imbedded in the rock. Landing here this afternoon, I found in the lower part of the escarpment a stratum of coal and forest trees, imbedded between strata of altered clay containing the remains of vegetables, the leaves of which indicate that the plants were dicotyledonous. Among these, the stems of some of the ferns are not mineralized, but merely charred, retaining still their vegetable structure and substance; and in this condition a portion also of the trees remain. The indurated appearance and compactness of the strata, as well, perhaps, as the mineralized condition of the coal, are probably due to igneous action. Some portions of the coal precisely resemble in aspect the cannel coal of England, and, with the accompanying fossils, have been referred to the tertiary formation.

These strata appear to rest upon a mass of agglomerated rock, being but a few feet above the water of the river; and over them is the escarpment of perhaps eighty feet, rising gradually in the rear towards the mountains. The current was now very swift, and we were obliged to *cordelle* the boat along the left shore, where the bank was covered with large masses of rocks.

Night overtook us at the upper end of the island, a short distance below the cascades, and we halted on the open point. In the mean time the lighter canoes, paddled altogether by Indians, had passed ahead, and were out of sight. With them was the lodge, which was the only shelter we had, with most of the bedding and provisions. We shouted, and fired guns; but all to no purpose, as it was impossible for them to hear above the roar of the river; and we remained all night without shelter, the rain pouring down all the time. The old voyageurs did not appear to mind it much, but covered themselves up as well as they could, and lay down on the sand beach where they remained quiet until morning. The rest of us spent a rather miserable night; and, to add to our discomfort, the incessant rain extinguished our fires; and we were glad when at last daylight appeared, and we again embarked.

Crossing to the right bank, we *cordelled* the boat along the shore, there being no longer any use for the paddles, and put into a little bay below the upper rapids. Here we found the lodge pitched, and about twenty Indians sitting around a blazing fire within, making a luxurious breakfast with salmon, bread, butter, sugar, coffee, and other provisions. In the forest, on the edge of the high bluff overlooking the river, is an Indian grave yard, consisting of a collection of tombs, in each of which were the scattered bones of many skeletons. The tombs were made of boards, which were ornamented with many figures of men and animals of the natural size - from their appearance, constituting the armorial device by which, among Indians, the chiefs are usually known.

Dictionary definitions of cordelle: As a nown: A towline, especially as formerly used on Mississippi flatboars and keelboats. As a verb: To tow with or as with a cordelle.

The masses of rock displayed along the shores of the ravine in the neighborhood of the cascades are clearly volcanic products. Between this cove, which I called Grave-yard bay, and another spot of smooth water above, on the right, called Lüders bay, sheltered by a jutting-point of huge rocky masses at the foot of the cascades, the shore along the intervening rapids is lined with precipices of distinct strata of red and variously colored lavas, in inclined positions.

The names Lüder's bay and Grave-yard bay are not shown on modern maps. These bays no longer exist. The Bonneville and Dalles dams now cover one-time shallow places and rapids to a considerable depth. No dams exist further downstream than the Bonneville, and the river is slow moving and smooth from this dam to the ocean. The dam at The Dalles thoroughly covers up the feature implied by its name (i.e., water through a narrow opening) as observed by Fremont. Another dam is located upstream from The Dalles near the John Day river. These various dams provide a major part of the electrical power for the northwest. Considerable barge traffic now plies the Columbia carrying grain from eastern Oregon and Washington along with wood chips used in making paper. A series of locks gets barges past the various dams.

The masses of rock forming the point at Lüders bay consist of a porous trap, or basalt - a volcanic product of a modern period. The rocks belong to agglomerated masses, which form the immediate ground of the cascades and have been already mentioned as constituting a bed of cemented coglomerate rocks appearing at various planes along the river. Here they are scattered along the shores, and through the bed of the river, wearing the character of convulsion, which forms the impressive and prominent feature of the river at this place.

Whenever we came in contact with the rocks of these mountains, we found them volcanic, which is probably the character of the range; and at this time, two of the great snowy cones, Mount Regnier and St. Helens, were in action. On the 23d of the preceding November, St. Helens had scattered its ashes, like a light fall of snow, over the Dalles of the Columbia, 50 miles distant. A specimen of these ashes was given to me by Mr. Brewer, one of the clergymen at the Dalles.

> Regnier is now spelled Rainier. Mount St. Helens blew off 1300 feet of its top in the eruption of 1980. Its peak is now at 8365 feet. Although not visible from the surface of the Columbia river, it is possible that Fremont might later have mistaken Mt. Adams for Mt. St. Helens. Comparing the Preuss map to modern maps shows Mt. Adams approximately due north of The Dalles and not Mt. St. Helens. Mt. Adams rises to 12,276 feet. It is the second highest mountain in Oregon and Washington after Mt. Rainier at 14,410 feet. If Mt. Shasta at 14,162 feet is included, then Mt. Adams remains the third highest peak in the Pacific States from south of Lake Tahoe in California to the Canadian border. The Yakima Indian reservation is on the eastern flanks of Mt. Adams.

The lofty range of the Cascade mountains forms a distinct boundary between the opposite climates of the regions along its western and eastern bases. On the west, they present a barrier to the clouds of fog and rain which roll up from the Pacific ocean and beat against their rugged sides, forming the rainy season of the winter in the country along the coast. Into the brighter skies of the region along their eastern base, this rainy winter never penetrates; and at the Dalles of the Columbia the rainy season is unknown, the brief winter being limited to a period of about two months, during which the earth is covered with the slight snows of a climate remarkably mild for so high a latitude. The Cascade range has an average distance of about 130 miles from the sea coast. It extends far both north and south of the Columbia, and is indicated to the distant observer, both in course and position, by the lofty volcanic peaks which rise out of it, and which are visible to an immense distance.

During several days of constant rain, it kept our whole force laboriously employed in getting our barge and canoes to the upper end of the cascades. The portage ground was occupied by emigrant families; their thin and insufficient clothing, bare-headed and bare-footed children, attesting the length of their journey, and showing that they had, in many instances, set out without a due preparation of what was indispensable.

A gentleman named Lüders, a botanist from the city of Hamburg, arrived at the bay I have called by his name while we were occupied in bringing up the boats. I was delighted to meet at such a place a man of kindred pursuits; but we had only the pleasure of a brief conversation, as his canoe, under the guidance of two Indians, was about to run the rapids; and I could not enjoy the satisfaction of regaling him with a breakfast, which, after his recent journey, would have been an extraordinary luxury. All of his few instruments and baggage were in the canoe, and he hurried around by land to meet it at the Grave-yard bay; but he was scarcely out of sight, when by the carelessness of the Indians, the boat was drawn into the midst of the rapids, and glanced down the river, bottom up, with the loss of every thing it contained. In the natural concern I felt for his misfortune, I gave to the little cove the name of Lüders bay.

November 15. - We continued to-day our work at the portage.

About noon, the two barges of the express from Montreal arrived at the upper portage landing, which, for large boats, is on the right bank of the river. They were a fine-looking crew, and among them I remarked a fresh-looking woman and her daughter, emigrants from Canada. It was satisfactory to see the order and speed with which these experienced watermen effected the portage, and passed their boats over the cascades. They had arrived at noon, and in the evening they expected to reach Vancouver. These batteaus carry the express of the Hudson Bay Company to the highest navigable point of the north fork of the Columbia, whence it is carried by an overland party to lake Winipec, where it is divided - part going to Montreal, and part to Hudson bay. Thus a regular communication is kept up between three very remote points.

The Canadian emigrant was much chagrined at the change of climates and informed me that, only a few miles above, they had left a country of bright blue sky and a shining sun. The next morning the upper parts of the mountains which directly overlook the cascades were white with the freshly fallen snow, while it continued to rain steadily below.

Late in the afternoon we finished the portage, and embarking again, moved a little distance up the right bank, in order to clear the smaller rapids of the cascades, and have a smooth river for the next morning. Though we made but a few miles, the weather improved immediately; and though the rainy country and the cloudy mountains were close behind, before us was the bright sky; so distinctly is climate here marked by a mountain boundary

November 17. - We had today an opportunity to complete the sketch of that portion of the river down which we had come by night, and of which I will not give a particular description, which the small scale of our map would not illustrate. Many places occur along the river, where the stumps, or rather portions of the trunks of pine trees, are standing along the shore, and in the water, where they may be seen at a considerable depth below the surface, in the beautifully clear water. These collections of dead trees are called on the Columbia the *submerged forest* and are supposed to have been created by the effects of some convulsion which formed the cascades, and which, by damming up the river, placed these trees under water and destroyed them. But I venture to presume that the cascades are older than the trees; and as these submerged forests occur at five or six places along the river, I had an opportunity to satisfy myself that they have been formed by immense land slides from the mountains, which here closely shut in the river, and which brought down with them into the river the pines of the mountain. At one place, on the right bank, I remarked a place where a portion of one of these slides seemed to have planted itself, with all the evergreen foliage, and the vegetation of the neighboring hill, directly amidst the falling and yellow leaves of the river trees. It occurred to me that this would have been a beautiful illustration to the eye of a botanist.

Following the course of a slide, which was very plainly marked along the mountain, I found that in the interior parts the trees were in their usual erect position; but at the extremity of the slide they were rocked about, and thrown into a confusion of inclinations.

About 1 O'clock in the afternoon we passed a sandy bar in the river, whence we had an unexpected view of Mount Hood, bearing directly south by compass.

During the day we used oar and sail, and at night had again a delightful camping ground, and a dry place to sleep upon.

November 18. - The day again was pleasant and bright. At 10'clock we passed a rock island, on the right shore of the river, which the Indians use as a burial ground; and, halting for a short time, about an hour afterwards, at the village of our Indian friends, early in the afternoon we arrived again at the Dalles.

Carson had removed the camp up the river a little nearer to the hills, where the animals had better grass. We found every thing in good order, and arrived just in time to partake of an excellent roast of California beef. My friend Mr. Gilpin had arrived in advance of the party. His object in visiting this country had been to obtain correct information of the Walahmette settlements; and he had reached this point in his journey, highly pleased with the country over which he had travelled, and with invigorated health. On the following day he continued his journey, in our returning boats to Vancouver.

Miscellaneous Comments:

Before we start Chapter 3, concepts and practices in finding latitude from measurements with a sextant are worth understanding because these measurements are so critical to accurately determining Fremont's route. However, those who are more interested in the story line can skip this and go directly to Chapter 3.

The earth spins about its axis with the north pole pointed in a constant direction with respect to the stars. During the year the earth moves about the sun with its location in space changing by almost 200 million miles in 6 months time. But the stars are so far away that this distance makes no significant difference in measured directions (but not so for the planets). Stars appear to revolve around the north pole as the earth spins. If a star existed exactly at the true north pole, then it would always indicate not only direction to north, but also its altitude above the horizon would give latitude directly.

A sextant measures the angle between the horizon and a star or other heavenly body. At sea the horizon is defined by looking at it, with a small correction if you are standing appreciably above water level. A second correction accounts for diffraction as starlight enters the atmosphere. There is no correction when the star is directly above. The correction can exceed 5 minutes of arc at elevation angles below 11 degrees, which can lead to an error of about 6 statute miles if not corrected.

At night, an observer at sea cannot easily find the horizon and so star shots are not so common, being limited to the twilight hours. The sun is seen during the day (unless cloud cover prevents this) with the moon at night and sometimes also during the day. There is a special kind of sextant that contains a bubble as in a carpenter's level which serves as a virtual horizon. The angle to a star is measured by centering the star (or sun or moon) in the bubble. In calm seas, a bubble sextant works reasonably well. But typical pitching and rolling can severely limit measurement accuracy.. (The smaller and more random motions in an airplane and not quite so damaging.)

If the observer is on a stable platform such as Fremont had on the ground, a bubble sextant can give good results. Modern sextants of this kind are equipped with a battery and a light so that the bubble can be seen at night. Clearly, such things did not exist in 1843. Obviously, the horizon in a mountainous area cannot directly be observed. A way around this (other than by using a carpenter's level with its bubble) is to use a pool of water with the star's image showing in this pool and acting as an horizon. Ripples due to wind can be reduced if there is a thin coat of oil on the surface of the water. The altitude measured to the star is then twice the angle from the true horizon. Fremont made all of his sextant measurements this way - as "double angles."

If you know the angle between the true north pole and a star, then when the star is at its highest or lowest position, latitude becomes its altitude plus or minus the angle from the north pole as provided in suitable astronomical tables. A sequence of altitude measurements of the star when it is near an extreme position permits an average to be found which can result in an accurate estimate. When the star is midway between extreme positions, latitude is given directly.

Polaris, the North Star, is (today) somewhat less than one degree away from true north. The circle it defines about north is small. Without making a correction, a direct measurement can be in error by anything from zero to 56 minutes of arc (about 65 statute miles). In the case of the north star, a convenient pair of indicator stars tells you when Polaris is properly lined up, and these indicators also allow a proper correction factor to be calculated when Polaris is not in an extreme position. Figure 2.8 shows the arrangement of these "indicator" stars.

But there still remains a problem. The circle defined by Polaris changes year by year and can lead to errors if the star almanac is not updated every few years. The stars don't change. The problem is the precession in which the earth wobbles like a spinning top. Because all stars remain fixed with respect to one another, the change in the direction of Polaris is applied to all other stars alike. This consistency allows latitude to be determined using any star by measuring an extreme altitude, corrected from tables calculated to allow for precession. (Sighting on stars too near to the vertical or too close to the horizon should be avoided.)

This explanation is meant to give the reader assurance that Fremont's latitude measurements are fairly accurate and reliable. Errors can and do occur in longitude because the time relative to a reference observatory time was not known with sufficient precision. Measurements based on emersion do not easily give time to within a few seconds unless a relatively large telescope in a stable environment is employed. An error of twenty seconds in time equates to roughly five miles. This doesn't sound like much. But it is enough to show a path in a valley or along a stream other than that supposed.

Most efforts to improve celestial navigation over the years have been for applications at sea. Except when ships are near harbors or reefs, or for high-flying aircraft, accuracies to better than a few miles may not be serious. But this is too much on land. Today, very accurate values can be obtained using Loran or the newest, Global Positioning System (GPS). The "bible" for navigation at sea (and air) is "The American Practical Navigator," Nathanial Bowditch, Defense Mapping Agency Hydrographic/Topographic Center, Bethesda, Maryland. This manual is Issued every year and upgraded with the latest information. The original by Bowditch was published in 1799. (Yes, 1799.) Immersion and emersion are not mentioned in the book. Figure 2.8 is from the Bowditch book.

CAPTIONS FOR MULTI-PART FIGURES

Figure 2.1. Three segments. This is the Preuss map from the Columbia River south through Pyramid Lake. Numbers in circles correspond to points of interest described in Figure 1.1.

Figure 2.2. Six segments. The first four are from the Oregon State road map from the Columbia River south to the border of California. Size reduced from the original. The last two parts are from the Nevada State road map from the border of California to somewhat south of Pyramid Lake. The scale differs from that for Oregon. Marks at segment boundaries clarify places where the segments of the various maps join. Large circles designate locations where Fremont made astronomical observations. Smaller circles fill in the route between these points and are based partly on the author's estimates.

Figure 2.3. Six segments. Aviation WAC chart (CF-16). Reduced from the original. Covers from the Columbia River south to Pyramid Lake. Large and small circles have the same significance as in Figure 2.2 and should be located at the same places.

Figures 2.4 to 2.8 are captioned with the illustrations.

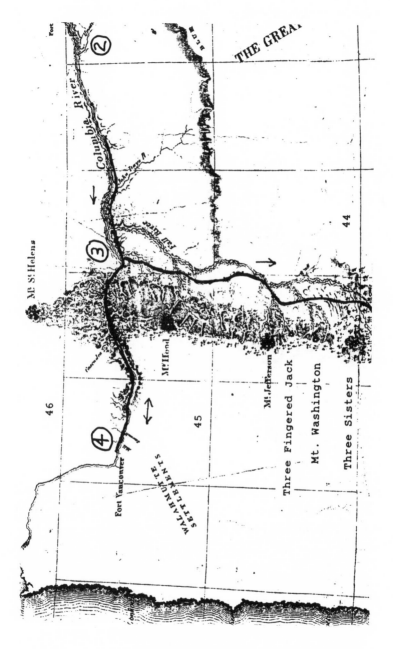

Figure 2.1-a

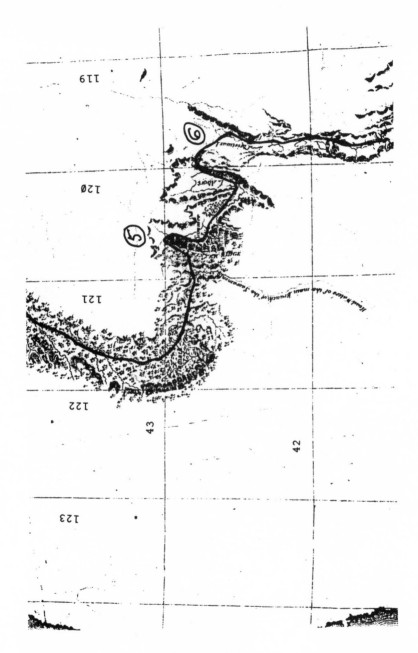

Figure 2.1-b

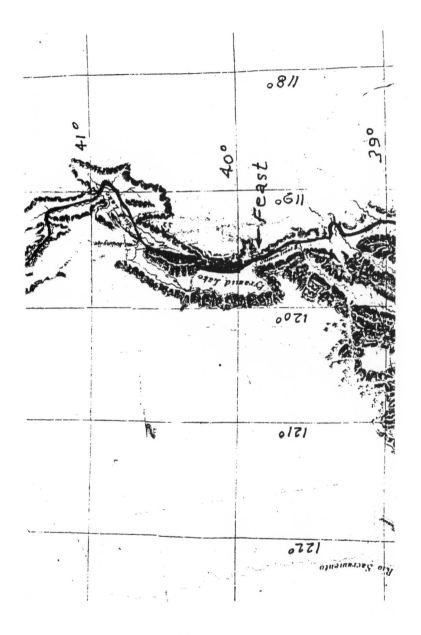

Figure 2.1-c

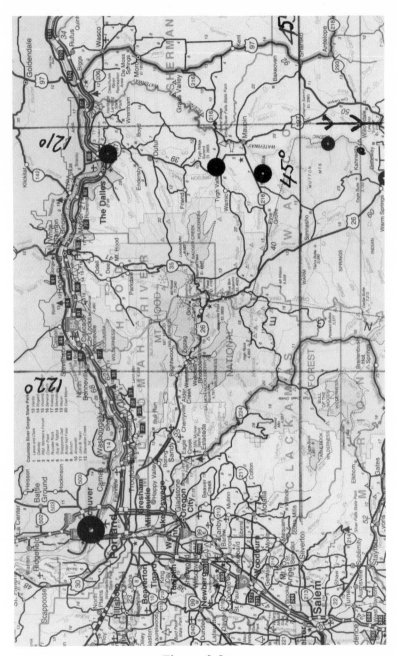

Figure 2.2-a

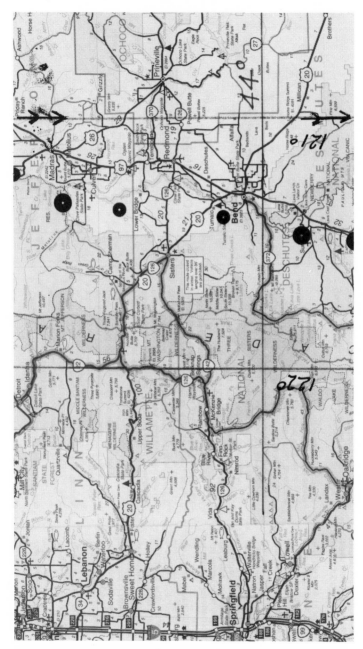

Figure 2.2-b

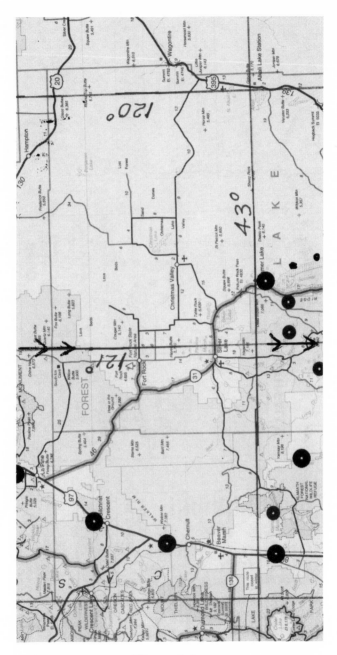

Figure 2.2-c

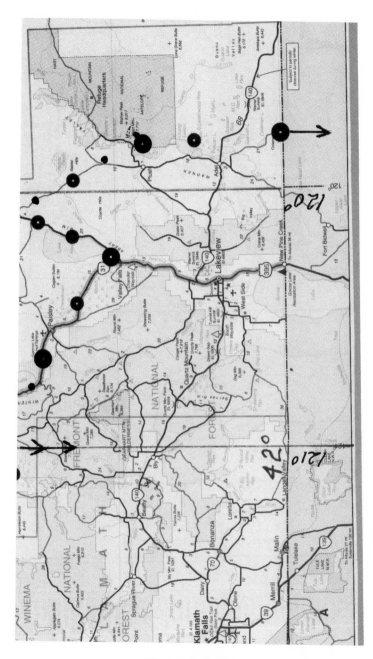

Figure 2.2-d

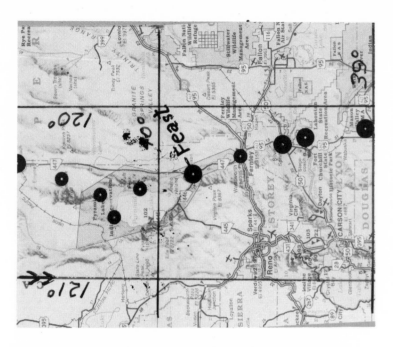

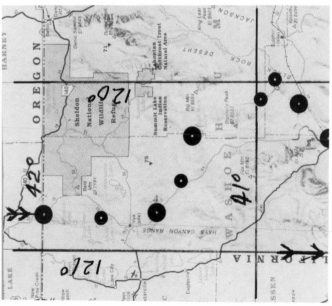

Figure 2.2-e

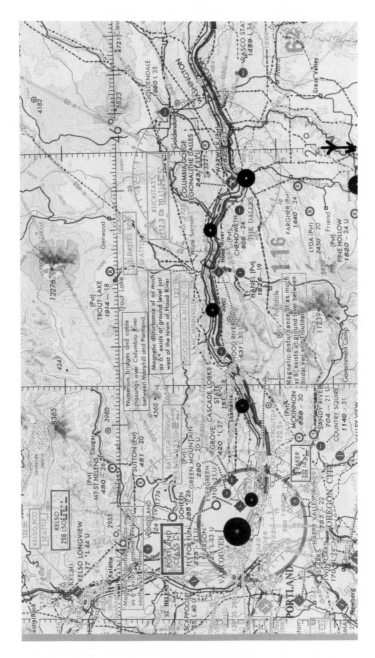

Figure 2.3-a

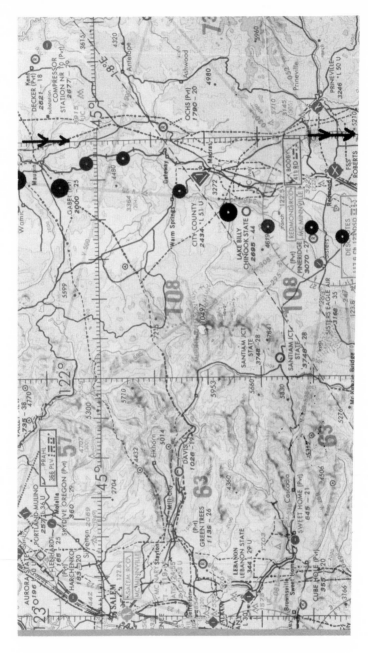

Figure 2.3-b

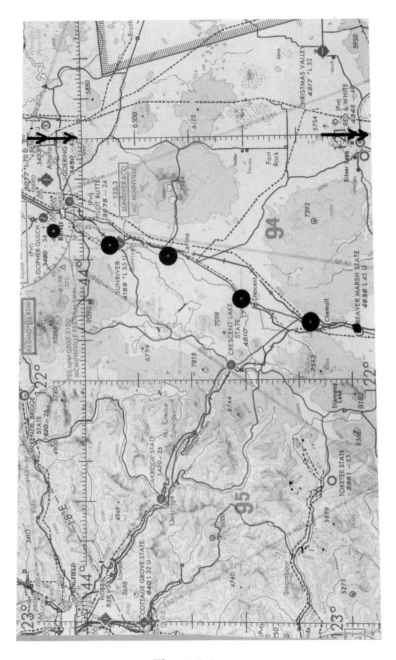

Figure 2.3-c

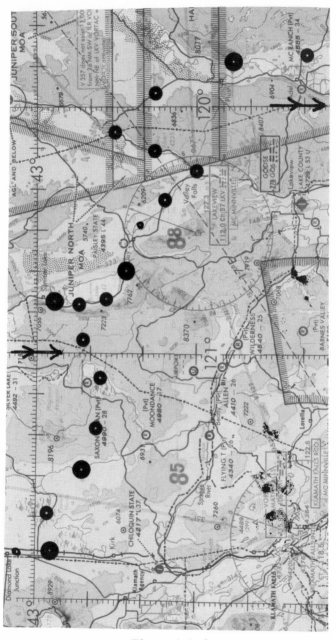

Figure 2.3-d

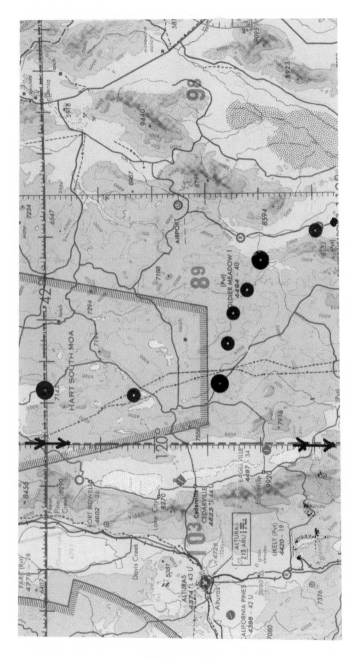

Figure 2.3-e

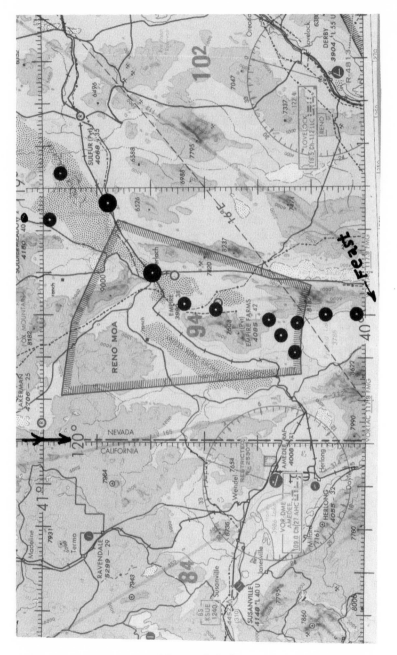

Figure 2.3-f

Figure 2.4. Multnomah Falls.

Figure 2.5. Beacon Rock.

Figure 2.6. Cape Horn from South Bank.

Figure 2.7. Part of restored Fort Vancouver.

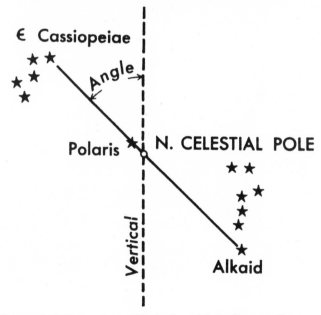

Figure 2.8. Star plot of Polaris with Indicator Stars.

Notes on Fremont's Guides

Christopher (Kit) Carson, 1809-1868. Frontiersman, trapper, soldier, and Indian agent. His meeting with Fremont in 1842 changed his life from an ordinary man to a celebrity. He remained with Fremont and was involved in the Bear Flag rebellion and transfer of California to the United States. He was noted for his fairness and sympathy for the plight of the Indians which led to his appointment as Indian agent in Taos, New Mexico, in 1854. He fought in the Civil war (as a Colonel) under General Stephen Kearney. He was appointed superintendent of Indian affairs for the Colorado territory but died shortly thereafter (of an aneurysm). Carson was illiterate. He dictated his memoirs in 1856. See the book "Dear Old Kit," H. L. Carter, 1968. (In 1998, vandals desecrated his grave in Taos with complaints that he killed Indians. The perpetrator was ignorant of his real respect for native Americans and that, in the early days, it was either kill or be killed.)

Thomas Fitzpatrick (1799-1854) was a mountain man, guide, and Indian agent. Coming from Ireland, he entered the fur trade in 1825. He guided wagon trains over the Oregon Trail as early as 1841. Fremont chose him as his guide (co-guide after Carson joined the group). He was the guide for General Kearney in 1846 when California was wrested from Mexico. He respected and was sympathetic to Indians. He negotiated major peace treaties with them in 1851 and 1853. He died of pneumonia in 1854.

Joseph R. Walker (1798-1876) explored much of the desert country in California and Nevada. He opened the Salt Lake-Humbolt trail which became the most important trail for subsequent immigrants. He traveled through the Owens Valley of California and discovered the Walker Pass, Yosemite Valley, and the giant redwood trees, all in the time period 1832-1834. Walker continued to guide emigrant groups to the west, even into old age. He served as a guide on the later part of Fremont's 1843-44 journey.

CHAPTER 3: TO SUMMER LAKE

Introduction:

In this chapter we begin to describe a true journey of discovery. In going south from The Dalles on the east side of the Cascade mountains, Fremont was travelling through lands not before seen by white men. Indeed, one or two brave trappers and scouts had crossed the region from east to west, but none had traversed the entire north-south path. Fremont extended this route to the south past Carson City, Nevada.

The route described in this chapter is shown on the maps of Figures 2.1, 2.2, and 2.3 of Chapter 2. These maps also include the journey to Lake Abert and south from there to Pyramid lake described is Chapter 4. The modern names of three mountains shown on the Preuss map have been added. Latitudes are generally fairly accurate. But longitudes have errors.

According to Fremont:

The camp was now occupied in making the necessary preparations for our homeward journey, which, though homeward, contemplated a new route, and a great circuit to the south and southeast, and the exploration of the Great Basin between the Rocky mountains and the *Sierra Nevada*. Three principal objects were indicated, by report or by maps, as being on this route; the character or existence of which I wished to ascertain, and which I assumed as landmarks or leading points on the projected line of return. The first of these points was the *Tlamath* lake, on the table land between the head of Fall river, which comes to the Columbia, and the Sacramento, which goes to the bay of San Francisco; and from which lake a river of the same name makes its way westwardly direct to the ocean. This lake and river are often called *Klamet*, but I have chosen to write its name according to the Indian pronunciation. The position of this lake, on the line of inland communication between Oregon and California; its proximity to the demarcation boundary of latitude 42 deg; its imputed double character of lake, or meadow, according to the season of the year; and the hostile and warlike character attributed to the Indians about it - all made it a desirable object to visit and examine. From this lake our course was intended to be about southeast, to a reported lake called Mary's, at some days' journey in the Great Basin and thence still on southeast, to the reputed *Buenaventura* river, which has had a place in so many maps, and countenanced the belief of the existence of a great river flowing from the Rocky mountains to the bay of San Francisco.

> Latitude 42 degrees is the present northern boundary of the State of California. The Tlamath Lake (Klamath today) consists of both an upper lake and a lower lake. The lower part is just within California. The upper lake, which is fairly large, is about 20 miles north of the California border. There also is a large Tlamath marsh about 20miles north of the upper lake. Fremont mistakes the marsh for the lake. He turns eastward from the marsh and thus never sees the actual lake.
> The myth, perpetrated on most maps of the day, that there exists a Mary's lake and a Buenaventura river giving water access from the rocky mountains to the pacific, is repeated here. Fremont's report later corrects these misconceptions. In his report, he appears to want the reader to follow the thoughts of the members of the expedition while they traveled, even though he later totally discredits these thoughts, along with old maps and myths.

From the Buenaventura the next point was intended to be in that section of the Rocky mountains which includes the heads of Arkansas river, and of the opposite waters of the Californian gulf; and thence down the Arkansas to Bent's fort, and home. This was our projected line of return a great part of it absolutely new to geographical, botanical, and geological science and the subject of reports in relation to lakes, rivers, deserts, and savages hardly above the condition of mere wild animals, which inflamed desire to know what this *terra incognita* really contained. It was a serious enterprise, at the commencement of winter, to undertake the traverse of such a region, and with a party consisting only of twenty-five persons, and they of many nations - American, French, German, Canadian, Indian, and colored - and most of them young, several being under twenty-one years of age. All knew that a strange country was to be explored, and dangers and hardships to be encountered; but no one blenched at the prospect. On the contrary, courage and confidence animated the whole party. Cheerfulness, readiness, subordination, prompt obedience, characterized all; nor did any extremity of peril and privation, to which we were afterwards exposed, ever belie, or derogate from, the fine spirit of this brave and generous commencement.

As he later reported, the homeward route deviated in a massive way from the one that was originally planned. This turned out to be fortunate for history, exploration, and the future acquisition of California by the United States. Fremont implies that corrections to his path and maps may be expected in the following paragraph.

The course of the narrative will show at what point, and for what reasons, we were prevented from the complete execution of this plan, after having made considerable progress upon it, and how we were forced by desert plains and mountain ranges, and deep snows, far to the southland near to the Pacific ocean, and along the western base of the Sierra Nevada; where, indeed, a new and ample field of exploration opened itself before us. For the present, we must follow the narrative, which will first lead us south along the valley of Fall river, and the eastern base of the Cascade range, to the Tlamath lake, from which, or its margin, three rivers go in three directions - one west to the ocean; another north, to the Columbia; the third south to California.

For the support of the party, I had provided at Vancouver, a supply of provisions for not less than three months, consisting principally of flour, peas, and tallo - the latter being used in cooking; and, in addition to this, I had purchased at the mission some California cattle, which were to be driven on the hoof. We had 104 mules and horses - part of the latter procured from the Indians about the mission; and for the sustenance of which, our reliance was upon the grass which we should find, and the soft porous wood, which was to be its substitute when there was none.

Mr. Fitzpatrick, with Mr. Talbot and the remainder of our party, arrived on the 21st; and the camp was now closely engaged in the labor of preparation. Mr. Perkins succeeded in obtaining as a guide to the Tlamath lake two Indians - one of whom, had been there, and bore the marks of several wounds he had received from some of the Indians in the neighborhood; and the other went along for company. In order to enable us to obtain horses, he despatched messengers to the various Indian villages in the neighborhood, informing them that we were desirous to purchase, and appointing a day for them to bring them in.

We made, in the mean time, several excursions in the vicinity. Mr. Perkins walked with Mr. Preuss and myself to the heights, about nine miles distant, on the opposite side of the river, whence, in fine weather, an extensive view may be had over the mountains, including seven great peaks of the Cascade range; but clouds, on this occasion, destroyed the anticipated pleasure, and we obtained bearings only to three that were visible: Mount Regnier, St. Helens, and Mount Hood. On the heights about one mile south of the mission, a very fine view may be had of Mount Hood and St. Helens. In order to determine their positions with as much accuracy as possible, the angular distances of the peaks were measured with the sextants, at different fixed points from which they could be seen.

I wish Fremont had made more bearing measurements and given the numbers in his report. Bearings should be with respect to true north and not compass north unless variation is always specified (because it differs over the surface of the earth). It is not difficult to determine variation by comparing compass north to the direction of the north star. The magnetic variation south of The Dalles is today a non-trivial 18 degrees east. Variation can change over the years.

The Indians brought in their horses at the appointed time and we succeeded in obtaining a number in exchange for goods; but they were relatively much higher here, where goods are plenty and at moderate prices, than we had found them in the more eastern part of our voyage. Several of the Indians inquired very anxiously to know if we had any *dollars*; and the horses we procured were much fewer in number than I had desired, and of thin, inferior quality; the oldest and poorest being those that were sold to us. These horses, as ever in our journey you will have occasion to remark, are valuable for hardihood and great endurance.

November 24. - At this place one of the men was discharged; and at the request of Mr. Perkins, a Chinook Indian, a lad of nineteen, who was extremely desirous to "see the whites," and make some acquaintances with our institutions, was received into the party under my special charge with the understanding that I would again return him to his friends. He had lived for some time in the household of Mr. Perkins, and spoke a few words of the English language.

November 25. - We were all up early, in the excitement of turning towards home. The stars were brilliant, and the morning cold - the thermometer at daylight 26 deg.

Our preparations had been finally completed, and to-day we commenced our journey. The little wagon which had hitherto carried the instruments I judged it necessary to abandon; and it was accordingly presented to the mission. In all our long travelling, it had never been overturned or injured by any accident of the road; and the only things broken were the glass lamps, and one of the front panels, which had been kicked out by an unruly Indian horse. The howitzer was the only wheeled carriage now remaining.

We started about noon, when the weather had become disagreeably cold, with flurries of snow. Our friend Mr. Perkins, whose kindness had been active and efficient during our stay, accompanied us several miles on our road; when he bade us farewell, and consigned us to the care of our guides.

Ascending to the uplands beyond the southern fork of the *Tinanens* creek, we found the snow lying on the ground in frequent patches, although the pasture appeared good, and the new short grass was fresh and green. We travelled over high, hilly land, and encamped on a little branch of *Tinanens* creek where there were good grass and timber. The southern bank was covered with snow, which was scattered over the bottom; and the little creek, its borders lined with ice, had a chilly and wintry look. A number of Indians had accompanied us so far on our road, and remained with us during the night. Two bad-looking fellows, who were detected in stealing, were tied and laid before the fire, and guard mounted over them during the night. The night was cold, and partially clear.

The name Tinanens creek no longer appears on maps. The one followed could be Threemile, Fivemile, or Eightmile. (Probably Threemile.)

November 26. - The morning was cloudy and misty and but a few stars visible. During the night water froze in the tents, and at sunrise the thermometer was at 20 deg. Left camp at 10 o'clock, the road leading along tributaries of the Tinanens, and being, so far, very good. We turned to the right at the fork of the trail, ascending by a steep ascent along a spur to the dividing grounds between this stream and the waters of Fall river. The creeks we had passed were timbered principally with oak and other deciduous trees. Snow lies every where here on the ground, and we had a slight fall during the morning; but towards noon the gray sky yielded to a bright sun. This morning we had a grand view of St. Helens and Regnier: the latter appeared of a conical form, and very lofty, leading the eye far up into the sky.

The line of the timbered country is very distinctly marked here, the bare hills making with it a remarkable contrast. The summit of the ridge commanded a fine view of the Taih prairie, and the stream running through it, which is a tributary to the Fall river, the chasm of which is visible to the right. A steep descent of a mountain hill brought us down into the valley, and we encamped on the stream after dark, guided by the light of fires, which some naked Indians belonging to a village on the opposite side were kindling for us on the bank. This is a large branch of the Fall river. There was a broad band of thick ice some fifteen feet wide on either bank, and the river current is swift and cold. The night was cold and clear, and we made our astronomical observation this evening with the thermometer at 20 deg.

> Modern maps do not show Taih prairie. However,
> they do show Tigh valley and Tigh ridge. But no prairie
> by the name of Tigh or Taih. Fremont has referred to Mt.
> Regnier (Rainier) which is near Settle, Washington.

In anticipation of coming hardships and to spare our horses, there was much walking done to-day; and Mr. Fitzpatrick and myself made the day's journey on foot. Somewhere near the mouth of this stream are the falls from which the river takes its name.

November 27. - A fine view of Mount Hood this morning; a rose-colored mass of snow, bearing S. 85 deg W. by compass. The sky is clear, and the air cold; the thermometer 2 deg .5 below zero; the trees and bushes glittering white, and the rapid stream filled with floating ice.

Stiletsi and *the White Crane*, two Indian chiefs who had accompanied us thus far, took their leave, and we resumed our journey at 10 o'clock. We ascended by a steep hill from the river bottom, which is sandy, to a volcanic plain, around which lofty hills sweep in a regular form. It is cut up by gullies of basaltic rocks, escarpments of which appear every where in the hills. This plain is called the Taih prairie, and is sprinkled with some scattered pines. The country is now far more interesting to a traveller than the route along the Snake and Columbia rivers. To our right we had always the mountains, from the midst of whose dark pine forests the isolated snowy peaks were looking out like giants. They served us for grand beacons to show the rate at which we advanced in our journey. Mount Hood was already becoming an old acquaintance, and, when we ascended the prairie, we obtained a bearing to Mount Jefferson, S. 23 deg W. The Indian superstition has peopled these lofty peaks with evil spirits, and they have never yet known the tread of a human foot. Sternly drawn against the sky, they look so high and steep, so snowy and rocky, that it would appear almost impossible to climb them; but still a trail would have its attractions for the adventurous traveller. A small trail takes off through the prairie, towards a low point in the range, and perhaps there is here a pass into the Walahmette valley.

Crossing the plain, we descended by a rocky hill into the bed of a tributary of Fall river, and made an early encampment. The water was in holes, and frozen over, and we were obliged to cut through the ice for the animals to drink. An ox, which was rather troublesome to drive, was killed here for food.

The evening was fine, the sky being very clear, and I obtained an immersion of the third satellite, with a good observation of an emersion of the first; the latter of which gives for the longitude, 121/02/43; the latitude, by observation, being 45/06/45. The night was cold - the thermometer during the observations standing at 9 deg.

Assuming latitude is correct, the longitude value appears to be in error. The map by Preuss shows the travel path west of Fall river. His value for longitude on a modern map shows location east of the river. The error is about 8 statute miles.

November 28. - The sky was clear in the morning, but suddenly clouded over, and at sunrise began to snow, with the thermometer at 18 deg.

We traversed a broken high country, partly timbered With pine, and about noon crossed a mountainous ridge, in which, from the rock occasionally displayed, the formation consists of compact lava. Frequent tracks of elk were visible in the snow. On our right, in the afternoon, a high plain, partially covered with pine, extended about ten miles, to the foot of the Cascade mountains.

At evening we encamped in a basin narrowly surrounded by rocky hills, after a day's journey of 21 miles. The surrounding rocks are either volcanic products, or highly altered by volcanic action, consisting of quartz and reddish-colored siliceous masses.

November 29. - We emerged from the basin, by a narrow pass, upon a considerable branch of Fall river, running to the eastward through a narrow valley. The trail, descending this stream, brought us to a locality of hot springs, which were on either bank. Those on the left, which were formed into deep handsome basins, would have been delightful baths, if the outer air had not been so keen, the thermometer in these being at 89 deg. There were others, on the opposite side, at the foot of an escarpment, in which the temperature of the water was 134 deg. These waters deposited around the spring a brecciated mass of quartz and feldspar, much of it of a reddish color.

At this point, he was almost exactly where the headquarters of the Warm Springs Indian Reservation is located today. The reservation belongs to a group of several tribes. The policy of the Tribal Council is one of conservation. The tribe's harvest of trees has been reduced so that trees will always be available for the future. When the number of salmon decreased by an excessive amount a few years ago, the tribe ceased fishing; and this was long before the state took action. They have instituted a senior center, wellness clinic, an early childhood educational center, and they provide support for the college bound. Their museum is nationally acclaimed. Activities carried out at the reservation provide a welcomed model for others.

We crossed the stream here, and ascended again to a high plain, from an elevated point of which we obtained a view of six of the great peaks - Mount Jefferson, followed to the southward by two others of the same class; and succeeding, at a still greater distance to the southward, were three other lower peaks, clustering together in a branch ridge. These, like the great peaks, were snowy masses, secondary only to them; and, from the best examination our time permitted, we are inclined to believe that the range to which they belong is a branch from the great chain, which here bears to the westward. The trail during the remainder of the day followed near to the large stream on the left, which was continuously walled in between high rocky banks. We halted for the night on a little by-stream.

The three peaks mentioned are the Three Sisters (at 44 degrees latitude). On the Preuss map, these and two more intermediate ones are not named. Modern names have been inserted. For those who aspire to climb mountains, we give the heights of the several peaks shown on the Preuss map. Mt. Hood, the tallest mountain in the State of Oregon, rises to 11,239. Mt. Jefferson 10,497. Three Fingered Jack 7,841. Mt. Washington 7,794. North, Middle, and South Sister 10,085, 10,047, and 10,358. Immediately adjacent to the Sisters is

Broken Top at 9,173 feet. A few miles south of this group of peaks is Mt. Bachelor, the popular ski resort, at 9,080 feet. When in the Klamath Marsh area, the Preuss map shows additional peaks, some of which ring Crater Lake.

November 30.- Our journey to-day was short. Passing over a high plain, on which were scattered cedars, with frequent beds of volcanic rock in fragments interspersed among the grassy grounds, we arrived suddenly on the verge of the steep and rocky descent to the valley of the stream we had been following, and which here ran directly across our path, emerging from the mountains on the right. You will remark that the country is abundantly watered with large streams, which pour down from the neighboring range.

These streams are characterized by the narrow and chasm-like valleys in which they run, generally sunk a thousand feet below the plain. At the verge of this plain, they frequently commence in vertical precipices of basaltic rock, and which leave only casual places at which they can be entered by horses. The road across the country, which would otherwise be very good, is rendered impracticable for wagons by these streams. There is another trail among the mountains, usually followed in the summer, which the snows now compelled us to avoid; and I have reason to believe that this, passing nearer the heads of these streams, would afford a much better road.

Figure 3.1 is a photograph of one of these chasms. At one of them, a plaque recognizes the passage of Fremont.

At such places, the gun carriage was unlimbered, and separately descended by hand. Continuing a few miles up the left bank of the river, we encamped early in an open bottom among the pines, a short distance below a lodge of Indians. Here, along the river the bluffs present escarpments seven or eight hundred feet in height, containing strata of a very fine porcelain clay, overlaid, at the height of about five hundred feet, by a massive stratum of compact basalt one hundred feet in thickness, which again is succeeded above by other strata of volcanic rocks. The clay strata are variously colored, some of them very nearly as white as chalk, and very fine grained. Specimens brought from these have been subjected to microscopical examination by Professor Bailey, of West Point, and are considered by him to constitute one of the most remarkable deposites of fluviatile infusoria on record. While they abound in genera and species which are common in fresh water, but which rarely thrive where the water is even brackish, not one decidedly marine form is to be found among them; and their fresh water origin is therefore beyond a doubt. It is equally certain that they lived and died at the situation where they were found, as they could scarcely have been transported by running waters without an admixture of sandy particles; from which, however, they are remarkably free. Fossil infusoria of a freshwater origin had been previously detected by Mr. Bailey in specimens brought by Mr. James O. Dana from the tertiary formation of Oregon. Most of the species in those specimens differed so much from those now living and known, that he was led to infer that they might belong to extinct species, and considered them also as affording proof of an alternation, in the formation from which they were obtained, of fresh and salt water deposites, which, common enough in Europe, had not hitherto been noticed in the United States. Coming evidently from a locality entirely different, our specimens* show very few species in common with those brought by Mr. Dana, but bear a much closer resemblance to those inhabiting the northeastern States. It is possible that they are from a more recent deposite; but the presence of a few remarkable forms which are common to the two localities renders it more probable that there is no great difference in their age.

The report gives one of the few footnotes at this point. The footnote, as it appears at the bottom of the text, reads:

* The specimens obtained at this locality are designated in the appendix by the Nos. 53, 54, 55, 56, 57, 58, 59 60. The results obtained by Mr. Bailey in his examination of specimens from the infusorial strata, with a plate exhibiting some of the most interesting forms, will be found imbodied in the appendix.

For those who are familiar with such things, Figure 3.2, from the appendix of Fremont's report, is reproduced.

I obtained here a good observation of an emersion of the second satellite; but clouds, which rapidly overspread the sky, prevented the usual number of observations. Those which we succeeded in obtaining are, however, good; and give for the latitude of the place 44/35/23, and for the longitude from the satellite 121/10/25.

December 1. - A short distance above our encampment, we crossed this river, which was thickly lined along its banks with ice. In common with all these mountain streams, the water was very clear, and the current swift. It was not every where fordable, and the water was three or four feet deep at our crossing, and perhaps a hundred feet wide. As was frequently the case at such places, one of the mules got his packs, consisting of sugar, thoroughly wet, and turned into molasses. One of the guides informed me that this was a "salmon water," and pointed out several ingeniously contrived places to catch the fish; among the pines in the bottom I saw an immense one, about twelve feet in diameter. A steep ascent from the opposite bank delayed us again; and as, by the information of our guides, grass would soon become very scarce, we encamped on the height of land, in a marshy place among the pines, where there was an abundance of grass. We found here a single Nez Percé family, who had a very handsome horse in their drove, which we endeavored to obtain in exchange for a good cow; but the man "had two hearts," or, rather, he had one and his wife had another: she wanted the cow, but he loved the horse too much to part with it. These people attach great value to cattle, with which they are endeavoring to supply themselves.

December 2. - In the first rays of the sun, the mountain peaks this morning presented a beautiful appearance, the snow being entirely covered with a hue of rosy gold. We travelled to-day over a very stony, elevated plain, about which were scattered cedar and pine, and encamped on another large branch of Fall river. We were gradually ascending to a more elevated region, which would have been indicated by the rapidly increasing quantities of snow and ice, had we not known it by other means. A mule which was packed with our cooking utensils wandered off among the pines unperceived, and several men were sent back to search for it.

December 3. - Leaving Mr. Fitzpatrick with the party, I went ahead with the howitzer and a few men, in order to gain time, as our progress with the gun was necessarily slower. The country continued the same - very stony, with cedar and pine; and we rode on until dark, when we encamped on a hill side covered with snow, which we used to-night for water, as we were unable to reach any stream.

December 4. - Our animals had taken the back track, although a great number were hobbled; and we were consequently delayed until noon. Shortly after we had left this encampment, the mountain trail from the Dalles joined that on which we were travelling. After passing for several miles over an artemisia plain, the trail entered a beautiful pine forest, through which we travelled for several hours; and about 4 o'clock descended into the valley of another large branch, on the bottom of which were spaces of open pines, with occasional meadows of good grass, in one of which we encamped. The stream is very swift and deep, and about 40 feet wide, and nearly half frozen over. Among the timber here, are larches 140 feet high, and over 3 feet in diameter. We had to-night the rare sight of a lunar rainbow.

December 5. - To-day the country was all pine forest, and beautiful weather made our journey delightful. It was too warm at noon for winter clothes; and the snow, which lay every where in patches through the forest, was melting rapidly. After a few hours' ride, we came upon a fine stream in the midst of the forest, which proved to be the principal branch of Fall river. It was occasionally 200 feet wide - sometimes narrowed to 50 feet; the waters very clear, and frequently deep. We ascended along the river, which sometimes presented sheets of foaming cascades; its banks occasionally blackened with masses of scoriated rock, and found a good encampment on the verge of an open bottom, which had been an old camping ground of the Cayuse Indians. A great number of deer horns were lying about, indicating game in the neighborhood. The timber was uniformly large; some of the pines measuring 22 feet in circumference at the ground, and 12 to 13 feet at six feet above.

In all our journeying, we had never travelled through a country where the rivers were so abounding in falls, and the name of this stream is singularly characteristic. At every place where we come in the neighborhood of the river, is heard the roaring of falls. The rock along the banks of the stream, and the ledge over which it falls, is a scoriated basalt, with a bright metallic fracture. The stream goes over in one clear pitch, succeeded by a foaming cataract of several hundred yards. In the little bottom above the falls, a small stream discharges into an entonnoir, and disappears below.

We had made an early encampment, and in the course of the evening Mr. Fitzpatrick joined us here with the lost mule. Our lodge poles were nearly worn out, and we found here a handsome set, leaning against one of the trees, very white, and cleanly scraped. Had the owners been here, we would have purchased them; but as they were not, we merely left the old ones in their place, with a small quantity of tobacco.

December 6. - The morning was frosty and clear. We continued up the stream on undulating forest ground, over which there was scattered much fallen timber. We met here a village of Nez Percé Indians, who appeared to be coming down from the mountains, and had with them fine bands of horses. With them were a few Snake Indians of the root-digging species. From the forest we emerged into an open valley ten or twelve miles wide, through which the stream was flowing tranquilly, upward of two hundred feet broad, with occasional islands, and bordered with fine broad bottoms. Crossing the river, which here issues from a great mountain ridge on the right, we continued up the southern and smaller branch, over a level country, consisting of fine meadow land, alternating with pine forests, and encamped on it early in the evening. A warm sunshine made the day pleasant.

December 7. - To-day we had good travelling ground; the trail leading sometimes over rather sandy soils in the pine forest, and sometimes over meadow land along the stream. The great beauty of the country in summer constantly suggested itself to our imaginations; and even now we found it beautiful, as we rode along these meadows, from half a mile to two miles wide. The rich soil and excellent water, surrounded by noble forests, make a picture that would delight the eye of a farmer; and I regret that the very small scale of the map would not allow us to give some representation of these features of the country.

I observed to-night an occultation of η *Geminorum*, which, although at the bright limb of the moon, appears to give a very good result, that has been adopted for the longitude. The occultation, observations of satellites, and our position deduced from daily surveys with the compass, agree remarkably well together, and mutually support and strengthen each other. The latitude of the camp is 43/30/36; and longitude, deduced from the occultation, 121/33/50.

The dictionary definition of occultation is a hiding; the state of being hidden; disappearance. In astronomy the dictionary defines the word to mean the disappearance of one heavenly body behind another. A solar eclipse is an occultation. In Fremont's case, it involved the moon passing in front of a star. The method is fraught with possible errors and in general requires a considerable amount of calculation. It is doubtful that Fremont made these calculations in the field. Rather, an effort to reduce data to location was probably made after his return.

December 8. - To-day we crossed the last branch of the Fall river, issuing, like all the others we had crossed, in a southwesterly direction from the mountains. Our direction was a little east of south, the trail leading constantly through pine forests. The soil was generally bare, consisting, in greater part, of a yellowish white pumice stone, producing varieties of magnificent pines, but not a blade of grass; and to-night our horses were obliged to do without food, and use snow for water. These pines are remarkable for the red color of the bolls; and among them occurs a species of which the Indians had informed me when leaving the Dalles. The unusual size of the cone (16 or 18 inches long) had attracted their attention; and they pointed it out to me among the curiosities of the country. They are more remarkable for their large diameter than their height, which usually averages only about 120 feet. The leaflets are short - only two or three inches long, and five in a sheath; the bark of a red color.

December 9. - The trail leads always through splendid pine forests. Crossing dividing grounds by a very fine road, we descended very gently towards the south. The weather was pleasant, and we halted late. The soil was very much like that of yesterday; and on the surface of a hill, near our encampment, were displayed beds of pumice stone; but the soil produced no grass, and again the animals fared badly.

December 10. - The country began to improve; and about 11 o'clock we reached a spring of cold water on the edge of a Savannah, or grassy meadow, which our guides informed us was an arm of the Tlamath lake; and a few miles further we entered upon an extensive meadow, or lake of grass, surrounded by timbered mountains. This was the Tlamath lake. It was a picturesque and beautiful spot, and rendered more attractive to us by the abundant and excellent grass, which our animals, after travelling through pine forests, so much needed; but the broad sheet of water which constitutes a lake was not to be seen. Overlooking it, immediately west, were several snowy knobs, belonging to what we have considered a branch of the Cascade range. A low point covered with pines made out into the lake, which afforded us a good place for an encampment, and for the security of our horses, which were guarded in view on the open meadow. The character of courage and hostility attributed to the Indians of this quarter induced more than usual precaution; and, seeing smokes rising from the middle of the lake (or Savannah) and along the opposite shores, I directed the howitzer to be fired. It was the first time our guides had seen it discharged; and the bursting of the shell at a distance, which was something like the second fire of the gun, amazed and bewildered them with delight. It inspired them with triumphant feelings, but on the camps at a distance the effect was different, for the smokes in the lake, and on the shores, immediately disappeared.

The Tlamath Marsh (Klamath) is now a wildlife preserve. A photograph of part of it is shown in Figure 3.3. As stated earlier, this is not Tlamath lake. The lake is some 20 miles further south and Fremont never saw it because he turned east at this point. Waters from the marsh flow to Tlamath lake which empties into Tlamath river. The river winds through mountains in the southern part of Oregon and then the northern part of California (well north of Mt. Shasta), finally empying into the sea about 30 miles south of the Oregon border.

The point on which we were encamped forms, with the opposite eastern shore, a narrow neck, connecting the body of the lake with a deep cove or bay which receives the principal stream, and scattered over the greater part of which the water (or rather ice) was at this time dispersed in shallow pools. Among the grass, and scattered over the prairie lake, appeared to be similar marshes. It is simply a shallow basin, which, for a short period at the time of melting snows is, covered with water from the neighboring mountains; but this probably soon runs off, and leaves for the remainder of the year a green Savannah, through the midst of which the river Tlamath, which flows to the ocean, winds its way to the outlet on the southwestern side.

December 11. - No Indians made their appearance, and I determined to pay them a visit. Accordingly, the people were gathered together, and we rode out towards the village in the middle of the lake which one of our guides had previously visited. It could not be directly approached, as a large part of the lake appeared a marsh; and there were sheets of ice among the grass, on which our horses could not keep their footing. We therefore followed the guide for a considerable distance along the forest; and then turned off towards the village, which we soon began to see was a few large huts, on the tops of which were collected the Indians. When we had arrived within half a mile of the village, two persons were seen advancing to meet us; and, to please the fancy of our guides, we ranged ourselves into a long line, riding abreast, while they galloped ahead to meet the strangers.

We were surprised, on riding up to find one of them a woman having never before known a squaw to take any part in the business of war. They were the village chief and his wife who, in excitement and alarm at the unusual event and appearance, had come out to meet their fate together. The chief was a very prepossessing Indian, with very handsome features, and a singularly soft and agreeable voice - so remarkable as to attract general notice.

The huts were grouped together on the bank of the river, which, from being spread out in a shallow marsh at the upper end of the lake, was collected here into a single stream. They were large round huts, perhaps 20 feet in diameter, with rounded tops, on which was the door by which they descended into the interior. Within, they were supported by posts and beams.

Almost like plants, these people seem to have adapted themselves to the soils and to be growing on what the immediate locality afforded. Their only subsistence at this time appeared to be a small fish, great quantities of which, that had been smoked and dried, were suspended on strings about the lodge. Heaps of straw were lying around; and their residence in the midst of grass and rushes had taught them a peculiar skill in converting this material to useful purposes. Their shoes were made of straw or grass, which seemed well adapted for a snowy country; and the women wore on their head a closely woven basket, which made a very good cap. Among other things, were parti-colored mats about four feet square, which we purchased to lay on the snow under our blankets, and to use for table cloths.

Numbers of singular-looking dogs, resembling wolves, were sitting on the tops of the huts; and of these we purchased a young one, which, after its birthplace, was named Tlamath. The language spoken by these Indians is different from that of the Shoshonee and Columbia river tribes; and otherwise than by signs they cannot understand each other. They made us comprehend that they were at war with the people who lived to the southward and to the eastward; but I could obtain from them no certain information. The river on which they live enters the Cascade mountains on the western side of the lake, and breaks through them by a passage impracticable for travellers; but over the mountains, to the northward, are passes which present no other obstacle than in the almost impenetrable forests. Unlike any Indians we had previously seen, these wore shells in their noses. We returned to our camp, after remaining here an hour or two, accompanied by a number of Indians.

In order to recruit a little the strength of our animals, and obtain some acquaintance with the locality, we remained here for the remainder of the day. By observation, the latitude of the camp was 42/56/51; and the diameter of the lake, or meadow, as has been intimated, about 20 miles; It is a picturesque and beautiful spot; and, under the hand of cultivation, might become a little paradise. Game is found in the forest; timbered and snowy mountains skirt it, and fertility characterizes it. Situated near the heads of three rivers, and on the line of inland communication with California, and near to Indians noted for treachery, it will naturally, in the progress of the settlement of Oregon, become a point for military occupation and settlement.

From Tlamath lake, the further continuation of our voyage assumed a character of discovery and exploration, which, from the Indians here, we could obtain no information to direct, and where the imaginary maps of the country, instead of assisting, exposed us to suffering and defeat. In our journey across the desert, Mary's lake, and the famous Buenaventura river, were two points on which I relied to recruit the animals, and repose the party. Forming, agreeably to the best maps in my possession, a connected water line from the Rocky mountains to the Pacific ocean, I felt no other anxiety than to pass safely across the intervening desert to the banks of the Buenaventura, where, in the softer climate of a more southern latitude, our horses might find grass to sustain them, and ourselves be sheltered from the rigors of winter and from the inhospitable desert. The guides who had conducted us thus far on our journey were about to return; and I endeavored in vain to obtain others to lead us, even for a few days, in the direction (east) which we wished to go. The chief to whom I applied alleged the want of horses, and the snow on the mountains across which our course would carry us, and the sickness of his family, as reasons for refusing to go with us.

December 12. - This morning the camp was thronged with Tlamath Indians from the southeastern shore of the lake; but, knowing the treacherous disposition which is a remarkable characteristic of the Indians south of the Columbia, the camp was kept constantly on its guard. I was not unmindful of the disasters which Smith and other travellers had met with in this country, and therefore was equally vigilant in guarding against treachery and violence.

> In his reference to Smith, Fremont is probably referring to the famed scout, trapper, and explorer, Jedediah Smith. Smith had troubles with Indians in the southwest and was killed as a young man in a later trip in northern climes. Smith is referred to again in Chapter 10 in connection with the naming of the Virgin River.

According to the best information I had been able to obtain from the Indians, in a few days' travelling we should reach another large water, probably a lake, which they indicated exactly in the course we were about to pursue. We struck our tents at 10 o'clock, and crossed the lake in a nearly east direction, where it has the least extension - the breadth of the arm being here only about a mile and a half. There were ponds of ice, with but little grass, for the greater part of the way; and it was difficult to get the pack animals across, which fell frequently and could not get up with their loads, unassisted. The morning was very unpleasant, snow falling at intervals in large flakes, and the sky dark. In about two hours we succeeded in getting the animals over; and, after travelling another hour along the eastern shore of the lake, we turned up into a cove where there was a sheltered place among the timber, with good grass, and we encamped. The Indians, who had accompanied us so far, returned to their village on the southeastern shore. Among the pines here, I noticed some five or six feet in diameter.

December 13. - The night has been cold; the peaks around the lake gleam out brightly in the morning sun, and the thermometer is at zero. We continued up the hollow formed by a small affluent to the lake, and immediately entered an open pine forest on the mountain. The way here was sometimes obstructed by fallen trees, and the snow was four to twelve inches deep. The mules at the gun pulled heavily, and walking was a little laborious. In the midst of the wood, we heard the sound of galloping horses, and were agreeably surprised by the unexpected arrival of our Tlamath chief, with several Indians. He seemed to have found his conduct inhospitable in letting the strangers depart without a guide through the snow, and had come, with a few others, to pilot us a day or two on the way. After travelling in an easterly direction through the forest for about four hours, we reached a considerable stream, with a border of good grass; and here, by the advice of our guides, we encamped. It is about thirty feet wide, and two to four feet deep; the water clear, with some current; and, according to the information of our Indians, is the principal affluent to the lake, and the head water of the Tlamath river.

A very clear sky enabled me to obtain here to-night good observations, including an emersion of the first satellite of Jupiter, which give for the longitude 121/20/42, and for the latitude 42/51/26. This emersion coincides remarkably well with the result obtained from an occultation at the encampment of December 7th to 8th, 1843; from which place, the line of our survey gives an easting of thirteen miles. The day's journey was 12 miles.

> That longitude values appeared to agree on different dates does not necessarily mean that the values are correct. They may be in error by the same amount. It is then implied that the chronometer did not gain or lose much time between the times when the two measurements were made.

December 14. - Our road was over a broad mountain, and we rode seven hours in a thick snow storm, always through pine forests, when we came down upon the head waters of another stream, on which there was grass. The snow lay deep on the ground, and only the high swamp grass appeared above. The Indians were thinly clad, and I had remarked during the day that they suffered from the cold. This evening they told me that the snow was getting too deep on the mountain, and I could not induce them to go any farther. The stream we had struck issued from the mountain in an easterly direction, turning to the southward a short distance below; and, drawing its course upon the ground, they made us comprehend that it pursued its way for a long distance in that direction, uniting with many other streams, and gradually becoming a great river. Without the subsequent information which confirmed the opinion, we became immediately satisfied that this water formed the principal stream of the *Sacramento* river; and, consequently, that this main affluent of the bay of San Francisco had its source within the limits of the United States, and opposite a tributary to the Columbia, and near the head of the Tlamath river, which goes to the ocean north of 42 degrees, and within the United States.

On the Preuss map of Figure 2.1 this stream is identified as the main branch of the Sacramento river. Actually, Fremont was on a marsh through which the Sycan river flows. About 20 miles south, this river empties into the Sprague river. The Sprague river empties into the upper Klamath lake. The Klamath river connects the lake to the Pacific ocean but somewhat south of the 42nd parallel, in California, rather than north of it. Modern charts show the marsh with the Sycan river, not the Sacramento river as shown on the Preuss map. The Preuss map has an error in longitude of about 7 minutes. Clearly, the myth of a waterway from the rockies to the Pacific was still believed, although Fremont learned the truth later on.

December 15. - A present, consisting of useful goods, afforded much satisfaction to our guides; and, showing them the national flag, I explained that it was a symbol of our nation; and they engaged always to receive it in a friendly manner. The chief pointed out a course, by following which we would arrive at the big water, where no more snow was to be found. Travelling in a direction N. 60 degrees E. by compass, which the Indians informed me, would avoid a bad mountain to the right, we crossed the Sacramento where it turned to the southward, and entered a grassy level plain - a smaller Grand Rond; from the lower end of which the river issued into an inviting country of low rolling hills. Crossing a hard-frozen swamp on the farther side of the Rond, we entered again the pine forest, in which very deep snow made our travelling slow and laborious. We were slowly but gradually ascending a mountain; and, after a hard journey of seven hours, we came to some naked places among the timber, where a few tufts of grass showed above the snow, on the side of a hollow; and here we encamped. Our cow, which every day got poorer, was killed here, but the meat was rather tough.

December 16. - We travelled this morning through snow about three feet deep, which, being crusted, very much cut the feet of our animals. The mountain still gradually rose; we crossed several spring heads covered with quaking asp; otherwise it was all pine forest. The air was dark with falling snow, which every where weighed down the trees. The depths of the forest were profoundly still; and below, we scarce felt a breath of the wind which whirled the snow through their branches. I found that it required some exertion of constancy to adhere steadily to one course through the woods, when we were uncertain how far the forest extended, or what lay beyond; and, on account of our animals, it would be bad to spend another night on the mountain.

Towards noon the forest looked clear ahead, appearing suddenly to terminate; and beyond a certain point we could see no trees. Riding rapidly ahead to this spot, we found ourselves on the verge of a vertical and rocky wall of the mountain. At our feet - more than a thousand feet below - we looked into a green prairie country, in which a beautiful lake, some twenty miles in length, was spread along the foot of the mountains, its shores bordered with green grass. Just then the sun broke out among the clouds, and illuminated the country below, while around us the storm raged fiercely. Not a particle of ice was to be seen on the lake, or snow on its borders, and all was like summer or spring. The glow of the sun in the valley below brightened up our hearts with sudden pleasure; and we made the woods ring with joyful shouts to those behind; and gradually, as each came up, he stopped to enjoy the unexpected scene. Shivering on snow three feet deep, and stiffening in a cold north winds, we exclaimed at once that the names of Summer Lake and Winter Ridge should be applied to these two proximate places of such sudden and violent contrast.

The names Summer Lake and Winter Ridge remain today. The forest through which they had traveled is today the Fremont National Forest. The view from the ridge is truly spectacular. The elevation of their viewpoint is 7135 feet. The lake is at 4147 feet, which is almost 3,000 feet below. (Fremont's initial estimate was only 1000 feet below.) The plaque at the location is shown in Figure 3.4. It reads:

SECOND FREMONT EXPLORING EXPEDITION OF 1843

You are standing at Fremont Point on top of Winter Ridge approximately 7,000 feet above sea level. Captain John C. Fremont of the U.S. Topographical Corps and his men arrived at this location on December 16, 1843. They were on a journey into the Great Basin Desert lands to the east. Captain Fremont led one of the first mapping parties through this part of Oregon. He and his party, including guide and frontiersman Kit Carson, traveled south from The Dalles on the Columbia River. This route took them through the Deschutes River valley, pine forests, mountain snows and rimrocks until reaching the exposed point you are currently standing on. Geographic and scientific knowledge of this area increased significantly as a result of Fremont's expedition.

To get to this place, take a gravel road from the highway just north of Summer lake. In about 20 miles you reach the viewpoint. The forest service has built a cabin close by, complete with large propane tank (but no electricity). It can be rented through the Fremont forest district near the town of Silver Lake. Just before our arrival, a newlywed couple had been staying there but had left and locked the place because of hordes of mosquitoes. The photograph of Figure 3.5 was taken from the viewpoint, looking eastward.

The view from the ridge signals a milestone in Fremont's travel. This was the first time he had actually seen the Great Basin from the west side. The basin includes south-central Oregon, most of Nevada, an eastern strip of northern California and much of California's Mojave desert, and much of Utah where it is bounded on its east side by the Great Salt Lake and modern Salt Lake City.

We were now immediately on the verge of the forest land, in which we had been travelling so many days; and, looking forward to the east, scarce a tree was to be seen. Viewed from our elevation, the face of the country exhibited only rocks and grass, and presented a region in which the artemisia became the principal wood, furnishing to its scattered inhabitants fuel for their fires, building material for their huts, and shelter for the small game which ministers to their hunger and nakedness. Broadly marked by the boundary of the mountain wall, and immediately below us, were the first waters of that Great Interior Basin which has the Wahsatch and Bear river mountains for its eastern, and the Sierra Nevada for its western rim; and the edge of which we had entered upwards of three months before, at the Great Salt lake.

At this point, Fremont begins to realize the extent of the great basin and that a river through it might not exist.

But he remains uncertain. A large blank area on the large Preuss map of 1845 represents the basin from which no waters reach the sea. This area bears the words on the map:

"THE GREAT BASIN: diameter 11 degrees of latitude, 10 degrees of longitude; elevation above the sea between 4 and 5000 feet surrounded by lofty mountains: contents almost unknown, but believed to be filled with rivers and lakes which have no communication with the sea, deserts and oases which have never been explored, and savage tribes, which no traveller has seen or described."

When we had sufficiently admired the scene below, we began to think about descending, which here was impossible, and we turned towards the north, travelling always along the rocky wall. We continued on for four or five miles, making ineffectual attempts at several places; and at length succeeded in getting down at one which was extremely difficult of descent. Night had closed in before the foremost reached the bottom, and it was dark before we all found ourselves together in the valley. There were three or four half dead dry cedar trees on the shore, and those who first arrived kindled bright fires to light on the others. One of the mules rolled over and over two or three hundred feet into a ravine, but recovered himself, without any other injury than to his pack; and the howitzer was left midway the mountain until morning. By observation, the latitude of this encampment is 42/57/22. It delayed us until near noon the next day to recover ourselves and put every thing in order; and we made only a short camp along the western shore of the lake, which in the summer temperature we enjoyed to-day, justified the name we had given it. Our course would have taken us to the other shore, and over the highlands beyond; but I distrusted the appearance of the country, and decided to follow a plainly beaten Indian trail leading along this side of the lake. We were now in a country where the scarcity of water and of grass makes travelling dangerous, and great caution was necessary.

December 18. - We continued on the trail along the narrow strip of land between the lake and the high rocky wall, from which we had looked down two days before. Almost every half mile we crossed a little spring, or stream of pure cool water; and the grass was certainly as fresh and green as in the early spring. From the white efflorescence along the shore of the lake, we were enabled to judge that the water was impure, like that of lakes we subsequently found; but the mud prevented us from approaching it. We encamped near the eastern point of the lake, where there appeared between the hills a broad and low connecting hollow with the country beyond. From a rocky hill in the rear, I could see, marked out by a line of yellow dried grass, the bed of a stream; which probably connected the lake with other waters in the spring.

The observed latitude of this encampment is 42/42/37.

The highway along the west side of Summer Lake has a rest stop with a plaque that gives the names of all of the members of Fremont's party. Figure 3.6 is a photograph of this plaque.

Figures 2.1, 2.2, and 2.3 of Chapter 2 plot Fremont's route from The Dalles to the camping spot on the south end of Summer Lake. These figures include the trip from there to Lake Abert and on to what they called Christmas lake, and then to Pyramid Lake. This part of the journey is the subject of Chapter 4.

Figure 3.1. A typical chasm.

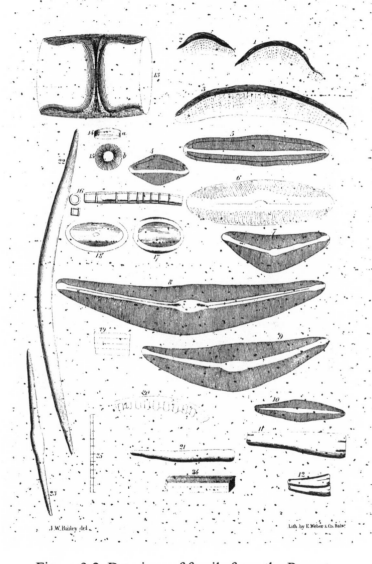

Figure 3.2. Drawings of fossils from the Report.

Figure 3.3. Sign at Klamath Marsh.

Figure 3.4. View of Summer Lake from Winter Ridge.

Figure 3.5. Plaque at Winter Ridge.

Figure 3.6. Fremont Memorial Plaque at Summer Lake.
The names of the men in his party are listed.

Brief Notes on Fremont

John Charles Fremont, 1813-1890, almost became our President. He was the first candidate for President to be nominated by the new Republican Party in 1856. He was defeated by James Buchanan by only 60 electoral votes. His loss might be related to his strong stand against slavery.

Events prior to this election show him to have been of great importance to the future of the nation. In 1846 a rag-tag group of Americans revolted against Mexico in the Bear Flag Revolt and created a new Republic. The action was instigated by Fremont. He was then appointed a major of a battalion by a navy man, Commodore Robert F. Stockton. Fremont accepted California's capitulation from Mexican officials in January, 1847. Stockton appointed him military governor. While this was in progress, General Stephen Kearney entered the southern part of California to complete the acquisition. An obvious conflict of interest ensued and Fremont was arrested and court-martialled in Washington D.C. for disobedience in a court action that remains today questionable. Sentenced to dismissal from the army, his penalty was set aside by Pres. James K. Polk. With bitterness, Fremont resigned from the military. Returning to California, he made and lost a fortune. Almost broke, he was appointed governor of the Arizona Territory in 1878, serving until 1883.

Many items bear Fremont's name besides geographical places. Fremont's squirrel of the Rocky Mountains is one. The Fremont cottonwood (*populus fremontii*) of the southwest part of North America is another. Fremontodendrumalso is known as the flannelbush. Fremont's pine, or Fremont's nut pine (*pinus monophyllas*) is common to the Western United States. Fremont is credited with naming the "Golden Gate" of San Francisco.

CHAPTER 4: THROUGH PYRAMID LAKE

Introduction:

This segment of Fremont's journey introduced him to a long stretch of desert, travelling south in Nevada not far from the California border. Even in this arid land, springs and meadows were found, although some nights were spent with little water or grass for animals. All of this segment lies within the Great Basin. Lakes may come and go with the seasons (dry lakes), leaving alkili residues. Mountains are barren with crags of volcanic origin. On the way, Fremont meets various Indian groups whose behavior in the presence of strangers suggests that some may never have seen white or black men. At the end of this segment, Fremont and his party feast, with Indians, on large salmon-trout (i.e., cutthroat trout) of exceptional quality.

According to Fremont:

December 19. - After two hours' ride in an easterly direction, through a low country, the high ridge with pine forest still to our right, and a rocky and bald but lower one on the left, we reached a considerable fresh-water stream, which issues from the piney mountains. So far as we had been able to judge, between this stream and the lake we had crossed dividing grounds; and there did not appear to be any connexion, as might be inferred from the impure condition of the lake water.

The rapid stream of pure water, roaring along between banks overhung with aspens and willows, was a refreshing and unexpected sight; and we followed down the course of the stream, which brought us soon into a marsh, or dry lake, formed by the expanding waters of the stream. It was covered with high reeds and rushes, and large patches of ground had been turned up by the squaws in digging for roots, as if a farmer had been preparing the land for grain. I could not succeed in finding the plant for which they had been digging. There were frequent trails, and fresh tracks of Indians; and, from the abundant signs visible, the black-tailed hare appears to he numerous here. It was evident that, in other seasons, this place was a sheet of water.

Crossing this marsh towards the eastern hills, and passing over a bordering plain of heavy sands, covered with artemisia, we encamped before sundown on the creek, which here was very small, having lost its water in the marshy grounds. We found here tolerably good grass. The wind to night was high, and we had no longer our huge pine fires but were driven to our old resource of small dried willows and artemisia. About twelve miles ahead, the valley appears to be closed in by a high, dark-looking ridge.

> Fremont frequently talks of artemisia. This is a very common bushy plant in temperate zones. It is usually referred to as sagebrush. A full-featured dictionary gives definitions for this plant as well as a number of others cited in the report.

December 20. - Travelling for few hours down the stream this morning, we turned a point of the hill on our left, and came suddenly in sight of another and much larger lake, which, along its eastern shore, was closely bordered by the high black ridge which walled it in by a precipitous face on this side. Throughout this region the face of the country is characterized by these precipices of black volcanic rock, generally enclosing the valleys of streams, and frequently terminating the hills. Often in the course of our journey we should be tempted to continue our road up the gentle ascent of a sloping hill, which, at the summit, would terminate abruptly in a black precipice. Spread out over a length of 20 miles, the lake, when we first came in view presented a handsome sheet of water; and I gave to it the name of Lake Abert, in honor of the chief of the corps to which I belonged.

The very beginning of the Report to Congress has it directed to Colonel J. J. Abert. The name given to the lake by Fremont remains today. The ridge to the east of the lake is now known as the Abert Rim. Figures 2.1, 2.2, and 2.3 in Chapter 2 show the route from Summer lake and around the lake on its eastern side so as to skirt the ridge, then south towards an area shown in continuing segments of these Figures. Figure 4.1 is a photograph of Abert Rim with the lake located over a slight rise on the left of the photograph. The remaining part of the route to Pyramid lake as described in this chapter is shown on the final segments of Figures 2.1, 2.2, and 2.3.

The fresh-water stream we had followed emptied into the lake by a little fall; and I was doubtful for a moment whether to go on, or encamp at this place. The miry ground in the neighborhood of the lake did not allow us to examine the water conveniently, and, being now on the borders of a desert country, we were moving cautiously. It was, however, still early in the day, and I continued on, trusting either that the water would be drinkable, or that we should find some little spring from the hill side. We were following an Indian trail which led along the steep rocky precipice; a black ridge along the western shore holding out no prospect whatever. The white efflorescences which lined the shore like a bank of snow, and the disagreeable odor which filled the air as soon as we came near, informed us too plainly that the water belonged to one of those fetid salt lakes which are common in this region.

We continued until late in the evening to work along the rocky shore, but, as often afterwards, the dry inhospitable rock deceived us; and, halting on the lake, we kindled up fires to guide those who were straggling along behind. We tried the water, but it was impossible to drink it, and most of the people to-night lay down without eating; but some of us, who had always a great reluctance to close the day without supper, dug holes along the shore, and obtained water, which, being filtered, was sufficiently palatable to be used, but still retained much of its nauseating taste. There was very little grass for the animals, the shore being lined with a luxuriant growth of chenopodiaceous shrubs, which burned with a quick bright flame, and made our firewood.

The next morning we had scarcely travelled two hours along the shore when we reached a place where the mountain made a bay, leaving at their feet a low bottom around the lake. Here we found numerous hillocks covered with rushes, in the midst of which were deep holes, or springs of pure water; and the bottom was covered with grass, which, although of salt and unwholesome quality, and mixed with saline efflorescences, was still abundant, and made a good halting place to recruit our animals; and we accordingly encamped here for the remainder of the day. I rode ahead several miles to ascertain if there was any appearance of a watercourse entering the lake; but found none, the hills preserving their dry character, and the shore of the lake sprinkled with the same white powdery substance, and covered with the same shrubs. There were flocks of ducks on the lake, and frequent tracks of Indians along the shore, where the grass had been recently burnt by their fires.

We ascended the bordering mountains in order to obtain a more perfect view of the lake in sketching its figure; hills sweep entirely around its basin, from which the waters have no outlet.

December 22. - To-day we left this forbidding lake. Impassable rocky ridges barred our progress to the eastward, and I accordingly bore off towards the south, over an extensive sage plain. At a considerable distance ahead, and a little on our left, was a range of snowy mountains, and the country declined gradually towards the foot of a high and nearer ridge immediately before us, which presented the feature of black precipices, now becoming common to the country. On the Summit of the ridge, snow was visible; and there being every indication of a stream at its base, we rode on until after dark, but were unable to reach it, and halted among the sage bushes on the open plain, without either grass or water. The two India rubber bags had been filled with water in the morning, which afforded sufficient for the camp; and rain in the night formed pools, which relieved the thirst of the animals. Where we encamped on the bleak sandy plain, the Indians had made huts or circular enclosures, about four feet high and twelve feet broad, of artemisia bushes. Whether these had been forts or houses, or what they had been doing in such a desert place, we could not ascertain.

> Travelling in a southerly direction, the ridges on his left now bear the names of Rabbit Hills, Hart Mountains, and Poker Jim Ridge. To his right was Coyote Hills and various mountains containing part of the Fremont National Forest. The ridge he cites as being immediately before him may be what is now called Flint Ridge. He is headed towards the Warner valley.

December 23. - The weather is mild; the thermometer at daylight 38 deg., the wind having been from the southward for several days. The country has a very forbidding appearance, presenting to the eye nothing but sage and barren ridges. We rode up towards the mountain, along the foot of which we found a lake, which we could not approach on account of the mud; and, passing around its southern end, ascended the slope at the foot of the ridge, where in some hollows we had discovered bushes and small trees - in such situations, a sure sign of water. We found here several springs and the hill side was well sprinkled with a species of *festuca* - a better grass than we had found for many days. Our elevated position gave us a good view over the country, but we discovered nothing very encouraging. Southward, about ten miles distant, was another small lake, towards which a broad trail led along the ridge; and this appearing to afford the most practicable route, I determined to continue our journey in that direction.

December 24. - We found the water of the lake tolerably pure, and encamped at the farther end. There were some good grass and canes along the shores and the vegetation at this place consisted principally of chenopodiaceous shrubs.

December 25. - We were roused, on Christmas morning, by a discharge from the small arms and howitzer, with which our people saluted the day; and the name of which we bestowed on the lake. It was the first time, perhaps, in this remote and desolate region, in which it had been so commemorated. Always, on days of religious or national commemoration our voyageurs expect some unusual allowance; and having nothing else I gave them each a little brandy, (which was carefully guarded, as one of the most useful articles a traveller can carry,) with some coffee and sugar, which here, where every eatable was a luxury, was sufficient to make them a feast.

> Fremont traveled southward just east of a string of dry and watered lakes known as the Warner Lakes. His value for latitude indicates that the particular lake named as Christmas lake is now called Hart Lake. There does exist a Christmas Lake and a Christmas Lake Valley about 30 miles due north of Summer Lake. But this is not the same and was not traversed by Fremont. Fremont's naming didn't get into the record books in this case.

The day was sunny and warm; and, resuming our journey, we crossed some slight dividing grounds into a similar basin, walled in on the right by a lofty mountain ridge. The plainly beaten trail still continued, and occasionally we passed camping grounds of the Indians, which indicated to me that we were on one of the great thoroughfares of the country. In the afternoon I attempted to travel in a more eastern direction; but, after a few laborious miles, was beaten back into the basin by an impassable country. There were fresh Indian tracks about the valley, and last night a horse was stolen. We encamped on the valley bottom, where there was some creamlike water in ponds, colored by a clay soil and frozen over. Chenopodiaceous shrubs constituted the growth, and made again our fire wood. The animals were driven to the hill, where there was tolerably good grass.

December 26. - Our general course was again south. The country consists of larger or smaller basins, into which the mountain waters run down, forming small lakes; they present a perfect level, from which the mountains rise immediately and abruptly. Between the successive basins, the dividing grounds are usually very slight; and it is probable that, in the seasons of high water, many of these basins are in communication. At such times there is evidently an abundance of water, though now we find scarcely more than the dry beds. On either side, the mountains, though not very high, appear to be rocky and sterile. The basin in which we were travelling declined towards the southwest corner, where the mountains indicated a narrow outlet; and, turning round a rocky point or cape, we continued up a lateral branch valley, in which we encamped at night on a rapid, pretty little stream of fresh water, which we found unexpectedly among the sage near the ridge, on the right side of the valley. It was bordered with grassy bottoms and clumps of willows, the water partially frozen. This stream belongs to the basin we had left. By a partial observation to-night, our camp was found to be directly on the 42d parallel. To night a horse belonging to Carson, one of the best we had in the camp, was stolen by the Indians.

At a latitude of 42 degrees and a longitude of 120 degrees, three states join together at a point, Oregon, California, and Nevada. Fremont was on the line separating Oregon and Nevada about 12 miles east of the California border. The creek he encamped upon may have been a tributary to one now called Twenty mile.

December 27. - We continued up the valley of the stream, the principal branch of which here issues from a bed of high mountains. We turned up a branch to the left, and fell into an Indian trail, which conducted us by a good road over open bottoms along the creek, where the snow was five or six inches deep. Gradually ascending, the trail led through a good broad pass in the mountain, where we found the snow about one foot deep. There were some remarkably large cedars in the pass, which were covered with an unusual quantity of frost, which we supposed might possibly indicate the neighborhood of water; and as, in the arbitrary position of Mary's lake, we were already beginning to look for it, this circumstance contributed to our hope of finding it near.

Descending from the mountain, we reached another basin, on the flat lake bed of which we found no water, and encamped among the sage on the bordering, plain, where the snow was still about one foot deep. Among this the grass was remarkably green, and to-night the animals fared tolerably well.

December 28. - The snow being deep, I had determined, if any more horses were stolen, to follow the tracks of the Indians into the mountains, and put a temporary check to their sly operations; but it did not occur again.

Our road this morning lay down a level valley, bordered by steep mountainous ridges, rising very abruptly from the plain. Artemisia was the principal plant, mingled with Fremontia and the chenopodiaceous shrubs. The artemisia was here extremely large, being sometimes a foot in diameter and eight feet high. Riding quietly along over the snow, we came suddenly upon smokes rising among these bushes; and, galloping up, we found two huts, open at the top, and loosely built of sage, which appeared to have been deserted at the instant; and, looking hastily around, we saw several Indians on the crest of the ridge near by, and several others scrambling up the side. We had come upon them so suddenly, that they had been wellnigh surprised in their lodges. A sage fire was burning in the middle; a few baskets made or straw were lying about, with one or two rabbit skins; and there was a little grass scattered about, on which they had been lying. "Tabibo - bo!" they shouted from the hills - a word which, in the Snake language, signifies *white* - and remained looking at us from behind the rocks. Carson and Godey rode towards the hills but the men ran off like deer. They had been so much pressed, that a woman with two children had dropped behind a sage bush near the lodge, and when Carson accidentally stumbled upon her, she immediately began screaming in the extremity of fear, and shut her eyes fast, to avoid seeing him. She was brought back to the lodge, and we endeavored in vain to open a communication with the men. By dint or presents, and friendly demonstrations, she was brought to calmness; and we found that they belonged to the Snake nation, speaking the language of that people.

Eight or ten appeared to live together, under the same little shelter; and they seemed to have no other subsistence than the roots or seeds they might have stored up, and the hares which live in the sage, and which they are enabled to track through the snow, and are very skilful in killing. Their skins afford them a little scanty covering. Herding together among bushes, and crouching almost naked over a little sage fire, using their instinct only to procure food, these may be considered, among human beings, the nearest approach to the mere animal creation. We have reason to believe that these had never before seen the face of a white man.

The day had been pleasant, but about two o'clock it began to blow; and crossing a slight dividing ground we encamped on the sheltered side of a hill, where there was good bunch grass, having made a day's journey of 24 miles. The night closed in, threatening snow; but the large sage bushes made bright fires.

December 29. - The morning mild, and at 4 o'clock it commenced snowing. We took our way across a plain, thickly covered with snow, towards a range of hills in the southeast. The sky soon became so dark with snow, that little could be seen of the surrounding country; and we reached the summit of the hills in a heavy snow storm. On the side we had approached, this had appeared to be only a ridge of low hills; and we were surprised to find ourselves on the summit of a bed of broken mountains, which, as far as the weather would permit us to see, declined rapidly to some low country ahead, presenting a dreary and savage character; and for a moment I looked around in doubt on the wild and inhospitable prospect, scarcely knowing what road to take which might conduct us to some place of shelter for the night.

Noticing among the hills the head of a grassy hollow, I determined to follow it, in the hope that it would conduct us to a stream. We followed a winding descent for several miles, the hollow gradually broadening into little meadows, and becoming the bed of a stream as we advanced; and towards night we were agreeably surprised by the appearance of a willow grove, where we found a sheltered camp, with water and excellent and abundant grass. The grass, which was covered by the snow on the bottom, was long and green, and the face of the mountain had a more favorable character in its vegetation, being smoother, and covered with good bunch grass. The snow was deep, and the night very cold. A broad trail had entered the valley from the right, and a short distance below the camp were the tracks where a considerable party of Indians had passed on horseback, who had turned out to the left, apparently with the view of crossing the mountains to the eastward.

> The route south of the 42nd parallel passed through the Sheldon National Antelope refuge, then past Massacre Lake to the camp where they spent two days. There are few roads in the general area, mostly of the unpaved kind suited for four wheel drive vehicles.

December 30. - After following the stream for a few hours in a southeasterly direction, it entered a canon where we could not follow; but determined not to leave the stream, we searched a passage below, where we could regain it, and entered a regular narrow valley. The water had now more the appearance of a flowing creek; several times we passed groves of willows, and we began to feel ourselves out of all difficulty. From our position, it was reasonable to conclude that this stream would find its outlet in Mary's lake, and conduct us into a better country. We had descended rapidly, and here we found very little snow. On both sides, the mountains showed often stupendous and curious-looking rocks, which at several places so narrowed the valley, that scarcely a pass was left for the camp. It was a singular place to travel through - shut up in the earth, a sort of chasm, the little strip of grass under our feet, the rough walls of bare rock on either hand, and the narrow strip of sky above. The grass to-night was abundant, and we encamped in high spirits.

December 31. - After an hour's ride this morning, our hopes were once more destroyed. The valley opened out, and before us again lay one of the dry basins. After some search, we discovered a high-water outlet, which brought us in a few miles, and by a descent of several hundred feet, into another long broad basin, in which we found the bed of a stream, and obtained sufficient water by cutting the ice. The grass on the bottoms was salt and unpalatable.

Here we concluded the year 1843, and our new year's eve was rather a gloomy one. The result of our journey began to be very uncertain; the country was singularly unfavorable to travel; the grasses being frequently of a very unwholesome character, and the hoofs of our animals were so worn and cut by the rocks, that many of them were lame, and could scarcely be got along.

Fremont's account is not too clear as to the exact route that he followed during this period. There were no longitude measures from December 16, 1843 through February 14, 1844. Latitude measures are given only every three or so days. These values are suspect because

it is not stated whether they were obtained at the start of
a day or at its end.

Fremont mentions a narrow canyon with a stream that
they could not directly follow. Rather, they followed it
on the rim of the canyon above. This canyon appears to
be Rock Creek Canyon. The creek flows into High Rock
Lake which borders a lower area that appears to be
where the new year was celebrated. The valley is
bordered on the west by the Calico Mountains and on the
east by the Black Rock Range. The extensive low lying
area is the Black Rock Desert.

New Year's Day, 1844. - We continued down the valley,
between a dry-looking black ridge on the left and a more
snowy and high one on the right. Our road was bad along
the bottom, being broken by gullies and impeded by sage,
and sandy on the hills, where there is not a blade of grass,
nor does any appear on the mountains. The soil in many
places consists of a fine powdery sand, covered with a
saline efflorescence; and the general character of the
country is desert. During the day we directed our course
towards a black cape, at the foot of which a column of
smoke indicated hot springs.

January 2. - We were on the road early, the face of the
country hidden by falling snow. We travelled along the bed
of the stream, in some places dry, in others covered with
ice; the travelling being very bad, through deep fine sand,
rendered tenacious by a mixture of clay. The weather
cleared up a little at noon, and we reached the hot springs
of which we had seen the vapor the day before. There was a
large field of the usual salt grass here, peculiar to such
places. The country otherwise is a perfect barren, without a
blade of grass, the only plants being some dwarf
Fremontias. We passed the rocky cape, a jagged broken
point, bare and torn. The rocks are volcanic, and the hills
here have a burnt appearance - cinders and coal
occasionally appearing as at a blacksmith's forge. We
crossed the large dry bed of a muddy lake in a southeasterly
direction, and encamped at night without water and without

grass, among sage bushes covered with snow. The heavy road made several mules give out to-day; and a horse, which had made the journey from the States successfully thus far, was left on the trail.

January 3. - A fog, so dense that we could not see a hundred yards, covered the country, and the men that were sent out after the horses were bewildered and lost; and we we consequently detained at camp until late in the day. Our situation had now become a serious one. We had reached and run over the position where, according to the best maps in my possession, we should have found Mary's lake, or river. We were evidently on the verge of the desert which had been reported to us; and the appearance of the country was so forbidding, that I was afraid to enter it, and determined to bear away to the southward, keeping close along the mountains, in the full expectation of reaching the Buenaventura river. This morning I put every man in the camp on foot - myself, of course, among the rest and in this manner lightened by distribution the loads of the animals. We travelled seven or eight miles along the ridge bordering the valley, and encamped where there were a few bunches of grass on the bed of a hill torrent, without water. There were some large artemisias; but the principal plants are chenopodiaceous shrubs. The rock composing the mountains is here changed suddenly into white granite. The fog showed the tops of the hills at sunset, and Stars enough for observations in the early evening, and then closed over us as before. Latitude by observation, 40/48/15.

> After passing the Calico Mountains, the party turned eastward into the Black Rock Desert. After almost 20 miles in this direction, they discovered the dismal appearance of the desert in front of them. They turned back to a southwest direction, travelling adjacent to mountains on the southeastern side of the desert.

January 4. - The fog to-day was still more dense, and the people again were bewildered. We travelled a few miles around the western point of the ridge, and encamped where there were a few tufts of grass, but no water. Our animals now were in a very alarming state, and there was increased anxiety in the camp.

January 5. - Same dense fog continued, and one of the mules died in camp this morning. I have had occasion to remark, on such occasions as these, that animals which are about to die leave the band, and, coming into the camp, lie down about the fires. We moved to a place where there was a little better grass, about two miles distant. Taplin, one of our best men, who had gone out on a scouting excursion, ascended a mountain near by, and to his great surprise emerged into a region of bright sunshine, in which the upper parts of the mountain were glowing, while below all was obscured in the darkest fog.

January 6. - The fog continued the same, and, with Mr. Preuss and Carson, I ascended the mountain, to sketch the leading features of the country, as some indication of our future route, while Mr. Fitzpatrick explored the country below. In a very short distance we had ascended above the mist, but the view obtained was not very gratifying. The fog had partially cleared off from below when we reached the summit; and in the southwest corner of a basin communicating with that in which we had encamped, we saw a lofty column of smoke, 16 miles distant, indicating the presence of hot springs. There, also, appeared to be the outlet of those draining channels of the country; and, as such places afforded always more or less grass, I determined to steer in that direction. The ridge we had ascended appeared to be composed of fragments of white granite. We saw here traces of sheep and antelope.

Entering the neighboring valley, and crossing the bed of another lake, after a hard day's travel over ground of yielding mud and sand, we reached the springs, where we found an abundance of grass, which, though only tolerably good, made this place, with reference to the past, a refreshing and agreeable spot.

His location at this time was near the present town of
Gerlach, Nevada. Water was available. Modern maps do
not show the hot springs..

This is the most extraordinary locality of hot springs we
had met during the journey. The basin of the largest one has
a circumference of several hundred feet; but there is at one
extremity a circular space of about fifteen feet in diameter,
entirely occupied by the boiling water. It boils up at
irregular intervals, and with much noise. The water is clear,
and the spring deep; a pole about sixteen feet long was
easily immersed in the centre, but we had no means of
forming a good idea of the depth. It was surrounded on the
margin with a border of *green* grass, and near the shore the
temperature of the water was 206 degrees. We had no
means of ascertaining that of the centre, where the heat was
greatest; but, by dispersing the water with a pole, the
temperature at the margin was increased to 208, and in the
centre it was doubtless higher. By driving the pole towards
the bottom, the water was made to boil up with increased
force and noise. There are several other interesting places,
where water and smoke or gas escape, but they would
require a long description. The water is impregnated with
common salt, but not so much so as to render it unfit for
general cooking; and a mixture of snow made it pleasant to
drink.

In the immediate neighborhood, the valley bottom is
covered almost exclusively with chenopodiaceous shrubs,
of greater luxuriance, and larger growth, than we have seen
them in any preceding part of the journey.

I obtained this evening some astronomical observations.

Our situation now required caution. Including those
which gave out from the injured condition of their feet, and
those stolen by Indians, we had lost, since leaving the
Dalles of the Columbia, fifteen animals; and of these, nine
had been left in the last few days. I therefore determined,
until we should reach a country of water and vegetation, to

feel our way ahead, by having the line of route explored some fifteen or twenty miles in advance, and only to leave a present encampment when the succeeding one was known.

Taking with me Godey and Carson, I made to-day a thorough exploration of the neighboring valleys, and found in a ravine in the bordering mountains a good camping place, where was water in springs, and a sufficient quantity of grass for a night. Overshading the springs were some trees of the sweet cottonwood, which, after a long interval of absence, we saw again with pleasure, regarding them as harbingers of a better country. To us, they were eloquent of green prairies and buffalo. We found here a broad and plainly marked trail, on which there were tracks of horses, and we appeared to have regained one of the thoroughfares which pass by the watering places of the country. On the western mountains of the valley, with which this of the boiling spring communicates, we remarked scattered cedars - probably an indication that we were on the borders of the timbered region extending to the Pacific. We reached the camp at sunset, after a day's ride of about forty miles. The horses we rode were in good order, being of some that were kept for emergencies, and rarely used.

Mr. Preuss had ascended one of the mountains, and occupied the day in sketching the country; and Mr. Fitzpatrick had found, a few miles distant, a hollow of excellent grass and pure water, to which the animals were driven, as I remained another day to give them an opportunity to recruit their strength. Indians appear to be every where prowling about like wild animals, and there is a fresh trail across the snow in the valley near.

Latitude of the boiling springs, 40/39/46.

On the 9th we crossed over to the cottonwood camp. Among the shrubs on the hills were a few bushes of *ephedra occidentalis*, which afterwards occurred frequently along our road, and, as usual, the lowlands were occupied with artemisia. While the party proceeded to this place,

Carson and myself reconnoitred the road in advance, and found another good encampment for the following day.

January 10. - We continued our reconnoisance ahead, pursuing a south direction in the basin along the ridge; the camp following slowly after. On a large trail there is never any doubt of finding suitable places for encampments. We reached the end of the basins where we found, in a hollow of the mountain which enclosed it, an abundance of good bunch grass. Leaving a signal for the party to encamp, we continued our way up the hollow, intending to see what lay beyond the mountain. The hollow was several miles long, forming a good pass, the snow deepening to about a foot as we neared the summit. Beyond, a defile between the mountains descended rapidly about two thousand feet; and, filling up all the lower space, was a sheet of green water, some twenty miles broad. It broke upon our eyes like the ocean. The neighboring peaks rose high above us, and we ascended one of them to obtain a better view. The waves were curling in the breeze, and their dark-green color showed it to be a body of deep water. For a long time we sat enjoying the view, for we had become fatigued with mountains, and the free expanse of moving waves was very grateful. It was set like a gem in the mountains, which, from our position, seemed to enclose it almost entirely. At the western end it communicated with the line of basins we had left a few days since; and on the opposite side it swept a ridge of snowy mountains, the foot of the great Sierra. Its position at first inclined us to believe it Mary's lake, but the rugged mountains were so entirely discordant with descriptions of its low rushy shores and open country, that we concluded it some unknown body of water; which it afterwards proved to be.

The route from the hot springs passed on the western flanks of the Selenite Range and then to the Lake Range. A pass between this range and the Fox Range was where the lake was first seen. Ending segments of Figures 2.1, 2.2, and 2.3 include this region.

On our road down, the next day, we saw herds of mountain sheep, and encamped on a little stream at the mouth of the defile, about a mile from the margin of the water, to which we hurried down immediately. The water is so slightly salt, that, at first, we thought it fresh, and would be pleasant to drink when no other could be had. The shore was rocky - a handsome beach, which reminded us of the sea. On some large granite boulders that were scattered about the shore, I remarked a coating of a calcareous substance, in some places a few inches and in others a foot in thickness. Near our camp, the hills, which were of primitive rock, were also covered with this substance, which was in too great quantity on the mountains along the shore of the lake to have been deposited by water, and has the appearance of having been spread over the rocks in mass.

A footnote gives an analysis of the composition of the rock. Fremont's comment is: "The label attached to a specimen of this rock was lost; but I append an analysis of that which, from memory, I judge to be the specimen."

Carbonate of lime	77.31
Carbonate of magnesia	5.25
Oxide of iron	1.60
Alumina	1.05
Silica	8.55
Organic matter, water, and loss	6.24
	100.00

Where we had halted, appeared to be a favorite camping place for Indians.

January 13. - We followed again a broad Indian trail along the shore of the lake to the southward. For a short space we had room enough in the bottom; but, after travelling a short distance, the water swept the foot of precipitous mountains, the peaks of which are about 3,000 feet above the lake. The trail wound along the base of these precipices, against which the water dashed below, by a way nearly impracticable for the howitzer. During a greater part of the morning the lake was nearly hid by a snow storm, and the waves broke on the harrow beach in a long line of foaming surf, five or six feet high. The day was unpleasantly cold, the wind driving the snow sharp against our faces; and, having advanced only about 12 miles, we encamped in a bottom formed by a ravine, covered with good grass, which was fresh and green.

We did not get the howitzer into camp, but were obliged to leave it on the rocks until morning. We saw several flocks of sheep, but did not succeed in killing any. Ducks were riding on the waves, and several large fish were seen. The mountain sides were crusted with the calcareous cement previously mentioned. There were chenopodiaceous and other shrubs along the beach; and, at the foot of the rocks, an abundance of *ephedra occidentalis*, whose dark-green color makes them evergreens among the shrubby growth of the lake. Towards evening the snow began to fall heavily, and the country had a wintry appearance.

The next morning the snow was rapidly melting under a warm sun. Part of the morning was occupied in bringing up the gun; and, making only nine miles, we encamped on the shore, opposite a very remarkable rock in the lake, which had attracted our attention for many miles. It rose, according to our estimate, 600 feet above the water; and, from the point we viewed it, presented a pretty exact outline of the great pyramid of Cheops. The accompanying drawing presents it as we saw it. Like other rocks along the shore, it seemed to be incrusted with calcareous cement. This striking feature suggested a name for the lake; and I called it Pyramid lake; and though it may be deemed by some a fanciful resemblance, I can undertake to say that the future traveller will find a much more striking resemblance between this rock and the pyramids of Egypt, than there is between them and the object from which they take their name.

Figure 4.2 is the sketch of the pyramid as presented in the report. The howitzer appears in the sketch. Figure 4.3 is a photograph from the opposite shore showing the pyramid, but much smaller due to distance. Today, no road goes along the eastern shore of the lake, and the entire region, including all of the lake, is the Pyramid Lake Indian Reservation. Figure 4.4 shows a plaque near the southern end of the lake.

The elevation of this lake above the sea is 4,890 feet, being nearly 700 feet higher than the Great Salt lake, from which it lies nearly west, and distant about eight degrees of longitude. The position and elevation of this lake make it an object of geographical interest. It is the nearest lake to the western rim, as the Great Salt lake is to the eastern rim, of the Great Basin which lies between the base of the Rocky mountains and the Sierra Nevada; and the extent and character of which, its whole circumference and contents, it is so desirable to know.

The last of the cattle which had been driven from the Dalles was killed here for food, and was still in good condition.

January 15. - A few poor-looking Indians made their appearance this morning, and we succeeded in getting one into the camp. He was naked, with the exception of a tunic of hare skins. He told as that there was a river at the end of the lake, but that he lived in the rocks near by. From the few words our people could understand, he spoke a dialect of the Snake language; but we were not able to understand enough to knew whether the river ran in or out, or what was its course; consequently, there still remained a chance that this might be Mary's lake.

Groves of large cottonwood, which we could see at the mouth of the river, indicated that it was a stream of considerable size and, at all events, we had the pleasure to know that now we were in a country where human beings could live. Accompanied by the Indian, we resumed our road, passing on the way several caves in the rock where there were baskets and seeds; but the people had disappeared. We saw also horse tracks along the shore.

Early in the afternoon, when we were approaching the groves at the mouth of the river, three or four Indians met us on the trail. We had an explanatory conversation in signs, and then moved on together towards the village, which the chief said was encamped on the bottom.

Reaching the groves, we found the *inlet* of a large fresh-water stream, and all at once were satisfied that it was neither Mary's river nor the waters of the Sacramento, but that we had discovered a large interior lake, which the Indians informed us had no outlet. It is about 35 miles long; and, by the mark of the water line along the shores, the spring level is about 12 feet above its present waters.

The chief commenced speaking in a loud voice as we approached; and parties of Indians armed with bows and arrows issued from the thickets. We selected a strong place for our encampment - a grassy bottom, nearly enclosed by the river, and furnished with abundant fire wood. The village, a collection of straw huts, was a few hundred yards higher up. An Indian brought in a large fish to trade, which we had the inexpressible satisfaction to find was a salmon trout; we gathered round him eagerly. The Indians were amused with our delight, and immediately brought in numbers; so that the camp was soon stocked. Their flavor was excellent - superior, in fact, to that of any fish I have ever known. They were of extraordinary size - about as large as the Columbia river salmon - generally from two to four feet in length. From the information of Mr. Walker, who passed among some lakes lying more to the eastward, this fish is common to the streams of the inland lakes. He subsequently informed me that he had obtained them weighing six pounds when cleaned and the head taken off, which corresponds very well with the size of those obtained at this place. They doubtless formed the subsistence of these people, who hold the fishery in exclusive possession.

I remarked that one of them gave a fish to the Indian we had first seen, which he carried off to his family. To them it was probably a feast; being of the Digger tribe, and having no share in the fishery, living generally on seeds and roots. Although this was a time of the year when the fish have not yet become fat, they were excellent, and we could only imagine what they are at the proper season. These Indians were very fat, and appeared to live an easy and happy life. They crowded into the camp more than was consistent with our safety, retaining always their arms; and, as they made some unsatisfactory demonstrations, they were given to understand that they would not be permitted to come armed into the camp; and strong guards were kept with the horses. Strict vigilance was maintained among the people, and one-third at a time were kept on guard during the night. There is no reason to doubt that these dispositions, uniformly preserved, conducted our party securely through Indians famed for treachery.

In the mean time, such a salmon-trout feast as is seldom seen was going on in our camp; and every variety of manner in which fish could be prepared - boiled, fried, and roasted in the ashes - was put into requisition; and every few minutes an Indian would be seen running off to spear a fresh one. Whether these Indians had seen whites before, we could not be certain; but they were evidently in communication with others who had, as one of them had some brass buttons, and we noticed several other articles of civilized manufacture. We could obtain from them but little information respecting the country. They made on the ground a drawing of the river, which they represented as issuing from another lake in the mountains three or four days distant, in a direction a little west of south; beyond which, they drew a mountain; and further still, two rivers; on one of which they told us that people like ourselves travelled. Whether they alluded to the settlements on the Sacramento, or to a party from the United States which had crossed the Sierra about three degrees to the southward, a few years since, I am unable to determine.

I tried unsuccessfully to prevail on some of them to guide us for a few days on the road, but they only looked at each other and laughed.

The latitude of our encampment, which may be considered the mouth of the inlet, is 39/51/13 by our observations.

Fremont gives to the river the name Salmon Trout. The modern name is Truckee River. The source of the river is in the Sierra Nevada mountains in the region of the famous (or infamous) Donner Pass. It flows through down town Reno, Nevada, and then eastward to a point more or less south of Pyramid lake. From there it flows north to the lake itself. The lake has no outlet to the sea.

The magnificent fish caught in this river may be a thing of the past. Indeed there may be trout, but huge ones are no longer so easy to find.

The Pyramid Indians, like many up and down the desert in this region, are collectively referred to as Paiutes. They remained relatively friendly until 1860 when miners raped two Indian women. This resulted in retribution when five white miners were killed. A rag-tag group of miners sought revenge but were defeated at the Big Bend of the Truckee river. Then a military operation of 800 civilians and army regulars tracked the Indians to Pinnacle Mountains where they were defeated. Fort Churchill was then established to guard the valley and keep the California trail open.

Other wars with the Paiutes were fought in different locations, at Coeur d'Alenes, Idaho in 1858-59, and the Snake wars in 1866-67.

For those in search of further information, contact Pyramid Lake Reservation, Pyramid Lake Paiute Tribal Counsel, Box 256, Nixon, NV 89424. (Tel:775-574-1000. Fax:574-1008.)

Figure 4.1. Abert Rim as seen from the fresh water stream. Lake Abert is over the rise to the left and beneath the rim. Unfortunately, time did not permit the author to follow Fremont's route on the east side of Aberrt lake. A future adventurer could readily follow this route.

Figure 4.2. The pyramid at Pyramid Lake.
From the Report.

Figure 4.3. Photograph of the pyramid
from the opposite shore.

PYRAMID LAKE

AMERICA'S MOST BEAUTIFUL DESERT LAKE IS A REMNANT OF ANCIENT LAKE
LAHONTAN WHICH DURING THE ICE AGE, COVERED SOME 8,450 SQUARE MILES
IN WESTERN NEVADA. CAVES AND ROCK SHELTERS ALONG ITS SHORE HAVE
YIELDED EVIDENCE OF A PREHISTORIC PEOPLE WITH A WELL-DEVELOPED COMMUNITY
LIFE.

JOHN C. FREMONT CAME UPON THE LAKE ON JANUARY 10, 1844 AND NAMED IT
FOR THE PYRAMID-SHAPED ISLAND JUST OFF THE EAST SHORE. THE PYRAMID
LAKE INDIAN RESERVATION WAS CREATED IN 1859. THE HISTORY OF THE PAIUTE
PEOPLE LIVING HERE HAS BEEN "ONE OF CONTENTION WITH THE WHITE MAN.
WITH THE INDIAN VICTORY IN THE FIRST BATTLE OF PYRAMID LAKE, MAY 12, 1860,
MORE WHITE MEN DIED THAN IN ANY PRIOR WHITE-INDIAN ENGAGEMENT IN THE
FAR WEST.

ANAHO ISLAND, JUST TO THE SOUTH OF THE PYRAMID, WAS ESTABLISHED AS
A NATIONAL WILDLIFE REFUGE IN 1913 AND IS TODAY ONE OF THE LARGEST
WHITE PELICAN NESTING GROUNDS IN NORTH AMERICA.

Figure 4.4. Plaque at Pyramid Lake.

CHAPTER 5: SAVAGES

For this final chapter, we change the way that our words are distinguished from those of the report because almost none of it comes from Fremont. The chapter starts with a few comments pertaining to Fremont's achievements in defining the nature of the land. The principal topic of this chapter concerns the nature of hunter-gatherer Indian tribes and why some were more "savage" than others. Fremont's observations match those of other explorers.

The path followed by Fremont added to our knowledge of the West in three important ways. First, it defined the limits of the Great Basin and put to rest several myths about nonexistent rivers, lakes, and whirlpools. Second, it described Utah in a way that enticed Mormons to settle there. And third, perhaps the most important of all, it described the West to the general public in a way that speeded and enhanced mass migration to the area. This in turn led to the claim on the territory by the United States only a few years later.

Perhaps one of the most interesting aspects of the report relates to the way that Fremont and his party interfaced with Native Americans and how he described the way that these tribal people lived and carried on commerce. Few reports exist today that detail Indian culture at and before the time that Europeans established more than very occasional contact with them. There were no horses or guns. Lack of animals to pull wagons provided no incentive for inventing the wheel. Except for limited areas in the southwest pueblo region, Indians did not farm. They were hunter-gatherer "savages."

Until the early 1800's, Europeans had made little contact with Indians beyond the Rocky Mountains north of where Spanish conquistadors and Missionaries traveled. Nor had "white man's diseases" yet decimated tribal populations. Some groups had horses as a legacy of Spanish presence, and many horses had escaped to form wild herds. Many tribes west of the Rocky mountains, especially in desert regions, had no need for horses because of the difficulty of maintaining them in a hot and dry environment or because people stayed close to food supplies in rivers or the sea.

In his travels, Fremont met and negotiated with several Indian groups that appeared to be living as they always had, without significant interactions with Europeans. Some of these were dangerous, warlike, dirty, poor, and treacherous. We hear nothing of this side of Indian culture today - it may be politically incorrect to repeat such stories. But ignoring such things ignores history.

We must not fault the Indians for behaving as savages. Hunter-gatherer cultures throughout the world behave in similar ways, just as Europeans in the North did before the Roman conquest. Surveys of the life styles of savages tend to point out achievements and other laudable acts while virtually ignoring things that we abhor. Fortunately, early explorers such as Captains Cook and Vancouver as well as several French and Spanish adventurers did provide some realistic information.

In his second edition, published in 1803, T. R. Malthus describes the checks to continued growth of populations in many parts of the world. The first volume of two volumes reprinted more recently (in 1952) is entirely given to a methodical presentation of these checks, from savages (below the level of the American Indian) to what was then considered to be a modern culture. Although his objective was not to describe cultures, he could not avoid doing so in order to present his thesis. He makes repeated reference to the reports of Cook's three voyages, that of Vancouver, Robertson's "History of America," and Burke's "America." He even uses information provided by Benjamin Franklin.

Fremont's report gives no hint as to whether or not he was aware of the writings of Malthus or the reports by explorers from which Malthus obtained his data. Fremont describes interactions with Indians tribes at several points in his report. Understanding what Fremont confronted was rather remarkably described by Malthus some 40 years before. Although the present book is not meant to be a treatise on Malthus and his ideas, it will nevertheless be useful to quote him directly.

All societies of hunter-gatherers displayed savage behavior to their neighbors. Women were generally treated as slaves. Babies were often exposed. Periodic famine was common. Crowded and dirty living standards promoted disease. Some tribes practiced cannibalism, especially during periods of famine. This practice in some cases led to a culture that embodied eating the flesh of one's opponents even when starvation was not the issue. The reader may recall what Fremont learned from Mr. Payette at Fort Boise (in Chapter 1). There were strong indications of cannibalism.

About women, Malthus says:

"In every part of the world, one of the most general characteristics of the savage is to despise and degrade the female sex. Among most of the tribes in America their condition is so peculiarly grievous that servitude is a name too mild to describe their wretched state. A wife is no better than a beast of burden. While a man passes his days in idleness or amusement, the woman is condemned to incessant toil. Tasks are imposed upon her without mercy, and services are received without complacence or gratitude. There are some districts in American where this state of degradation has been so severely felt that mothers have destroyed their female infants to deliver them at once from a life in which they were doomed to such a miserable slavery."

This state of servitude is not entirely general as Malthus reports:

"Among some of the tribes seated on the banks of rivers well stored with fish, or others that inhabit a territory greatly abounding in game or much improved in agriculture, the women are more valued and admired; and as hardly any restraint is imposed on the gratification of desire, the dissoluteness of their manners is sometimes excessive."

We don't single out Indians as being especially nasty in their habits. All hunter-gatherers display similar behavior. In fact, many North American Indians were not as vicious as their counterparts in other parts of the world.

Graduating from the lowest stage to the point where farming and herding are practiced does not preclude misery from excessive population relative to available resources; for in times of famine brought on by drought or cataclysms of other kinds, the worst in human behavior again is revealed. The higher population densities of pastoral groups leads to even greater suffering in bad times and also encourages plagues.

Some Indians of Central and South America farmed, but virtually no agriculture was practiced north of the southern parts of the present states of Arizona and New Mexico. Lands either were heavily forested, very dry and foreboding, or rolling grassy plains. If Indians happened to live near a river or the sea, much of their food could be obtained as fish. But often this was a seasonal thing with hunger during part of the year. It may seem strange to us today that many tribes failed to put aside food for use during seasons of want, but this is what Malthus reports. And this is also what Mr. Payette at Fort Boise told Fremont. (See Chapter 1.) Further examples of this kind of improvidence are apparent to Malthus when desert and mountain tribes are encountered after leaving Pyramid Lake.

The specific question that Malthus seeks to answer is the way that populations are maintained more or less constant in order to match numbers with the amount of available food. In forested lands, a considerable area is needed to support a single Indian family. Except for a few animals (deer, etc.), food must be obtained from roots and nuts and whatever else is edible including insects and grubs. Population densities are small. In the desert there is even less food available per unit area than in forests with even smaller population densities. Many explorers have reported long stretches of land in which no humans could be seen. This is consistent with a quite small population density.

Malthus reports that Indian women do not produce as many children as they could. Some reasons for this are cited. At one point, Malthus even mentions abortion:

"The state of depression and constant labour, added to the unavoidable hardships of savage life, must be very unfavourable to the office of child-bearing; and the libertinage which generally prevails among the women before marriage, with the habit of procuring abortions, must necessarily render them more unfit for bearing children afterwards. One of the missionaries, speaking of the common practice among the Natchez of changing their wives, adds, unless they have children by them; a proof that many of these marriages were unfruitful, which may be accounted for from the libertine lives of the women before wedlock, which he had previously noticed."

The warlike nature of Indians stems from a desire to keep outsiders away from their own vital food-providing areas, or from a desire to acquire areas from others because their own needs had increased. However, warrior leaders were careful to avoid loss of their own troops; for if their numbers were decimated, a group of Indians from another tribe could take over their lands and kill their women and children judged to be excessive in numbers. Fremont frequently comments on the "treacherous" nature of Indian war parties. A typical ploy would be to befriend the explorers and then, when their guard was down, attack them mercilessly. Fremont was aware of this practice which is why he kept his group ever ready and sought the best camping places from the point of view of defense. Not wanting to waste warriors, the Indians would generally not press an attack against a properly fashioned "fort" (where the word is used for any encampment). Fremont was well aware of the experience of Jededia Smith and others when friendliness turned to treachery.

Malthus says:

"The odds of ten to one are necessary to warrant an attack on a person who is armed and prepared to resist; and even then each is afraid of being the first to advance. The great object of the most renowned warrior is by every art of cunning and deceit, by every mode of stratagem and surprise that his invention can suggest, to weaken and destroy the tribes of his enemies with the least possible loss to his own. To meet an enemy on equal terms is regarded as extreme folly. To fall in battle, instead of being reckoned as an honourable death, is a misfortune, which subjects the memory of a warrior to the imputation of rashness and imprudence. But to lie in wait day after day, till he can rush upon his prey when most secure, and least able to resist him, to steal in the dead of night upon his enemies, set fire to their huts, and massacre the inhabitants, as they fly naked and defenceless from the flames, are deeds of glory, which will be of deathless memory in the breasts of his grateful countrymen."

In many ways, the words of Malthus are as important today as they were when he first set them down. The old days of misery are not gone. They prevail today in parts of Africa, the middle east, the Indian sub-continent, Latin America, Southeast Asia, and even in Europe where people are now being slaughtered, babies exposed, long-term residents expelled, and women and children sold into slavery. Practices of "ethnic cleansing" and genocide are by no means a thing of the past! In almost all cases, such practices come from shortages and demands by the people for help from their leaders. People with full bellies do not lust for the resources of their neighbors!

See T.R. Malthus, "On the Principle of Population." Everyman's Library, London: J.M Dent & Sons, Ltd. New York: E.P. Dutton & Co., Inc. First published 1914 with reprints thereafter. The original work by Malthus was published anonymously in 1798. The second edition, under his name, came in 1803.

The Darwin Connection

Malthus presents 22 chapters outlining checks to population in 22 different regions and countries in the world. The chapter on American Indians is only one of these. But it contains two critical paragraphs that could have been the ones that inspired Charles Darwin and A. Russel Wallace to finalize theories of natural selection and survival of the fittest. In the introduction to the book cited above, W. T. Layton gives a direct quote by Darwin. This is repeated here followed by the crucial paragraphs in the Malthus essay of 1803. First from Darwin's autobiography:

"In October 1838, that is fifteen months after I had begun my systematic inquiry, I happened to read for amusement Malthus on Population, and being well prepared to appreciate the struggle for existence which everywhere goes on, from long-continued observation in the habits of animals and plants, it at once struck me that under these circumstances favourable variations would tend to be preserved and unfavourable ones to be destroyed."

It almost can be argued that Malthus first stated the theory in shortened form. The following two paragraphs from Malthus are:

"As the parents are frequently exposed to want themselves, the difficulty of supporting their children becomes at times so great that they are reduced to the necessity of abandoning or destroying them. Deformed children are very generally exposed; and among some of the tribes in South America, the children of mothers who do not bear their labour well, experience a similar fate, from a fear that the offspring may inherit the weakness of its parents."

"To causes of this nature we must ascribe the remarkable exemption of the Americans from deformities of make. Even when a mother endeavours to rear all her children without distinction, such a proportion of the whole number perishes under the rigorous treatment which must be their lot in the savage state, that probably none of those who labour under any original weakness or infirmity can attain the age of manhood. If they be not cut off as soon as they are born, they cannot long protract their lives under the severe discipline that awaits them. In the Spanish provinces, where the Indians do not lead so laborious a life, and are prevented from destroying their children, great number of them are deformed, dwarfish, mutilated, blind, and deaf."

APPENDIX

LATITUDES AND LONGITUDES WITH PLACES AND DATES
May, 1843 to July, 1844
Degrees/minutes/seconds

Date	Latitude	Longitude	Place	Corrected Long.
May --- 1843				
30	38/49/41	94/25/31	Elm Grove	
June				
1	39/01/16	95/11/09	Small trib. to Kan	
4	39/11/17	95/66/30	Buck creek trib.	
5	39/08/24	96/06/02	Elk creek trib.	
10	39/03/38	96/24/56	Smokey Hill fork	
12	39/22/12	97/05/32	Trib. Repub. fork	
15	39/32/54	98/11/41	Trib. Repub. fork	
17	39/37/38	98/46/50	Trib. Salmon fork	
19	39/42/35	99/22/03	Trib. Salmon fork	
22	39/53/59	100/31/30	Trib. Repub. fork	
23	39/49/28	100/52/00	Prairy Dog river	
25	40/05/08	102/44/47	Camp, small lake	
30	40/31/02	103/23/29	So. fork Platte R.	
July				
1	40/17/21	104/02/00	So. fork above Beav.	
7	39/43/53	105/24/34	So. fork cherry cr.	
15	38/15/23	104/58/30	Ark and Boil sprngs	
18	38/52/10	105/22/45	Boiling springs	
21	39/41/45	105/25/38	South fork	
23	40/16/52	105/12/23	St. Vrain's fort	
30	41/02/19	105/35/17	High prairie	
31	41/04/06	-----	Near above	
31	41/15/02	106/16/54	Laramie river	
August				
1	41/23/08	-----	Stream to lake	
2	41/45/59	-----	Fork of Laramie	
2	41/37/16	106/47/25	Medicine Bow river	
3	41/35/48	-----	Trib. North fork	
5	41/35/59	107/22/27	No. fork Platte R.	
8	42/02/03	-----	High plateau	
9	-----	107/50/07	Sweet Water R.	
10	42/31/17	-----	Sweet Water R.	

13	42/19/53	-----	Sandy fork Green R.
13	42/18/08	109/25/55	Trib. Little Sandy
14	42/15/11	-----	Little Sandy R.
15	41/53/54	110/05/05	Green R. left bank
16	41/46/54	-----	Green R. trade post
16	41/37/38	110/10/28	Black's fork Green
17	41/29/53	110/25/06	Black's fork
18	41/26/08	110/45/58	Trib. Ham's fork
19	41/34/24	-----	Muddy R Ham's fork
20	41/39/45	-----	Muddy river
21	41/53/55	-----	Bear river
21	42/03/47	111/10/53	Bear river
22	42/10/27	-----	Bear R, Thomas fork
24	42/29/05	-----	Tullick's fork Bear
24	42/36/56	111/42/08	Bear river
25	42/39/57	111/46/00	Beer springs
29	42/07/18	-----	Pass entrance
30	42/14/22	-----	Roseaux or Reed riv
31	41/59/31	-----	Near Roseaux creek

Sept.

2	41/30/21	112/15/46	Bear R near mouth
3	41/30/22	112/19/30	Mouth of Bear R.
7	41/15/50	112/06/43	Weber's fork
8	41/11/26	112/11/30	Mouth Weber's fork
9	41/10/42	112/21/05	Island Salt Lake
10	41/14/17	-----	Halt in mud
12	41/15/50	112/06/43	Weber's fork
13	41/42/43	112/05/12	Bear R S. of gap
15	42/12/57	112/15/04	Roseaux or Reed R
17	42/44/40	112/29/52	Pannack river
21	43/01/30	112/29/54	Fort Hall
24	42/47/05	112/40/13	Snake above Amer.
28	42/29/57	-----	Snake river
29	42/26/21	114/06/04	Rock Cr. of Snake
30	42/38/44	114/25/04	Snake opp. spring

Oct.

1	42/40/11	114/35/12	Snake below fishing
2	42/53/40	114/53/04	Snake river
3	42/55/58	115/04/46	Ford at Snake R
7	43/35/21	115/54/46	Boisee river
8	43/40/53	116/22/40	Boisee river
10	43/49/22	116/47/03	Fort Boisee
12	44/17/36	116/56/45	Snake below Birch Cr.

14	44/37/44	117/09/49	Head of Burnt river	
15	44/50/32	117/24/21	Old bed of Powder R.	
16	44/59/29	117/29/22	Powder river	
18	45/26/47	117/28/26	Grand Rond	
19	45/38/07	117/28/34	East Blue Mountains	
23	45/53/35	118/00/39	Walahwalah foot mtns	
26	46/03/46	-----	Fort Nez Perce	
28	45/58/08	-----	Columbia left bank	
30	45/50/05	119/22/18	Columbia left bank	
31	45/44/23	119/45/09	Columbia left bank	

Nov.

5	45/35/55	120/55/00	Missionary at Dalles	121/10
5	45/35/31	120/53/51	Hills near mission	121/08
11	45/33/09	122/06/15	Rt bank below casc	122/00
26	45/14/24	-----	Large br of Fall R	121/10
27	45/06/45	121/02/43	South of Taih prairie	121/12
30	44/35/23	121/10/25	Main branch of Fall	121/18

Dec.

5	43/55/20	-----	Fall R (Union falls)	121/27
6	43/44/15	-----	Fall R (Union falls)	121/30
7	43/30/36	121/33/50	Fall R (Union falls)	121/40
8	43/17/49	-----	Camp in pines	121/46
10	42/56/51	-----	Tlamath lake	121/48
13	42/51/26	121/20/42	Trib. and Tlamath	121/28
16	42/57/22	-----	Summer lake	120/48
18	42/42/37	-----	Summer lake	120/40
24	42/23/25	-----	Christmas lake	119/48
26	42/00/09	-----	Desert valley	119/47
29	41/27/50	----	Camp to 30th	119/45
31	41/19/55	-----	New Year Eve camp	119/17

Jan. --- <u>1844</u>

3	40/48/15	-----	Near the Mud lake	119/02
6	40/39/46	-----	Near Great Boil Spr	119/20
15	39/51/13	-----	Pyramid lake, Salm R.	119/24
18	39/24/16	-----	River of Sierra	119/12
19	39/19/21	-----	River of Sierra	119/09
21	39/01/53	-----	River of Sierra	119/08
22	38/49/54	-----	River near gap	119/00
23	38/36/19	-----	Same river	118/58
24	38/24/28	-----	Head of stream	119/00
26	38/18/01	-----	Large stream	119/13
30	38/37/18	-----	Same as 18th-19th	119/31

Feb.

5	38/42/26	-----	First camp in pass	119/48
14	38/41/57	120/25/27	The Long camp	119/55
19	38/41/57	120/25/27	The Long camp	119/55
20	38/44/00	120/28/00	Summit of pass	119/58
24	38/46/58	120/34/20	Rio Americanos	120/09

Mar.

10	38/34/42	-----	Nueva Helvetia	121/25
22	38/34/42	-----	Neuva Helvetia	121/25
25	38/08/23	121/23/03	Mukelemnes R	121/12
26	38/02/48	121/16/22	Calaveras R	121/08
28	37/42/26	121/07/13	Stanislaus R	121/10
31	37/15/43*	120/46/30	Stanislaus R	120/46

April

3	37/22/05	120/58/03	Trib. San Joaquin	120/57
4	37/08/00	120/45/22	San Joaquin R	120/39
5	36/49/12	120/28/34	San Joaquin R	120/23
8	36/24/50	119/41/40	Lake fork (Tulares)	119/41
9	36/08/38	119/22/02	Stream to lake	119/19
10	35/49/10	118/56/34	Stream to lake	118/55
13	35/17/12	118/35/03	Near Pass creek	118/38
14	35/03/00	118/18/09	Stream E. Sierra	118/16
15	34/41/42	118/20/00	Rock spring	118/20
18	34/27/03	117/43/21	Springs foot mtn.	117/43
21	34/34/11	117/13/0	Mohahve R Span. Tr.	117/19
24	34/56/00	116/29/19	Mohahve R Span. Tr.	116/38
25	35/13/08	116/23/28	Agua de Tomaso	116/31
29	35/51/21	-----	Hernandez spring	116/13

May

1	35/58/19	-----	Deep spring in sands	115/56
3	36/10/20	-----	Las Vegas	115/15
5	36/38/56	-----	Br Rio Virgen	114/33
6	36/39/33	-----	Rio Virgen	114/19
8	36/53/03	-----	Rio Virgen	113/55
9	36/53/40	-----	Rio Virgen	113/53
12	37/28/28	-----	Vegas de Santa Clara	113/37
19	38/18/20	-----	Trib Sevier lake	112/39
23	39/22/19	-----	Sevier river	112/02
24	39/42/15	-----	St. Utah lake	111/52
27	40/04/27	-----	Right br. Span. fork	111/38
28	39/55/11	-----	Head Spanish fork	

| 29 | 40/00/07 | ----- | Head Uintah river |
| 30 | 40/18/52 | 112/18/30 | Duchesne fork |

June

3	40/27/45	109/56/42	Uintah fort
5	40/28/06	109/27/07	Ashley's fork
7	40/46/27	-----	Brown's Hole, Green
8	40/46/27	-----	Green in Brown's hole
10	41/01/48	-----	Elk Head river
11	41/01/11	-----	Elk Head river
13	41/18/48	-----	N. fork Platte
14	41/08/16	-----	N. fork Platte
15	40/52/44	-----	New Park
16	40/33/22	-----	New Park
19	39/57/26	-----	Old Park fork, Grand
22	39/20/24	-----	Bayou salade
26	38/39/22	-----	Small stream to Ark.
28	38/23/48	-----	Large stream to Ark.
29	38/15/23	-----	Ark. and Fontaine riv.

July

2	38/02/08	-----	Near Bent's fort
9	38/51/15	-----	Smoky Hill river
10	38/52/28	-----	Smoky Hill river
13	38/45/57	-----	Smoky Hill river
17	38/42/32	-----	Smoky below Pawnee
19	38/43/32	98/17/31	Smoky Hill river
21	38/28/38	-----	S. Smoky Hill fork
22	38/31/38	-----	Smlky Hill, Santa Fe
23	38/33/22	-----	Santa Fe road
28	38/46/50	98/04/34	Black jack. END.

Comments and errors:

Nov. 5. First entry, end of Chapter 1. Where the Deschutes
river empties into Columbia.

Nov. 11. No cross check. On way to Ft. Vancouver.

Nov. 27. Wapinita town.

Dec. 24. Hart lake.

Feb. 20. Given in text but not in this listing.

Mar. 31. Apparent misprint. Try 37/45/43.

Apr. 8. Kings river.

Apr. 29. Near Tecopa and Armagosa river.

May 1. Calvada or Charleston View. (Not on most maps.)

May 5 Muddy river (or Meadow Valley Wash).

May 30. Apparent misprint. Try 111/18/30.

TABLE OF DISTANCES
(The Dalles to Utah Lake only)

Date	Distance per day	Miles from start	Location (few given)
November, 1843			
11/25	12	12	
11/26	22	34	
11/27	13	47	
11/28	21	68	
11/29	21	89	
11/30	10	99	
December			
12/1	6	105	
12/2	11	118	
12/3	22	138	
12/4	9	147	
12/5	11	158	
12/6	19	177	
12/10	15	250	Tlamath lake
12/13	12	267	
12/14	21	288	
12/15	21	309	
12/16	9	318	Summer lake
12/17	6	324	
12/18	20	344	
12/19	21	365	
12/20	26	391	Lake Abert
12/21	6	397	
12/22	29	426	
12/23	7	433	
12/24	13	446	Christmas lake
12/25	14	460	
12/26	21	481	
12/27	24	505	
12/28	16	521	
12/29	15	536	
12/30	17	553	
12/31	18	571	
January, 1844			
1/1	20	591	
1/2	25	616	

1/3	7	623
1/4	7	630
1/5	2	632
1/6	15	647
1/9	11	658
1/10	10	668
1/11	10	678
1/12	6	684
1/13	12	696
1/14	9	705
1/15	12	717
1/16	18	735
1/17	22	757
1/18	8	765
1/19	18	783
1/20	5	788
1/21	24	812
1/22	14	826
1/23	25	851
1/24	20	871
1/25	25	896
1/27	12	308
1/28	12	920
1/29	7	927
1/30	11	938
1/31	26	694

February
2/2	16	980	
2/3	7	987	
2/4	3	990	
2/7	4	994	
2/8	1	995	
2/10	3	998	
2/20	3	1001	Sierra summit
2/21	5	1006	
2/22	3	1009	
2/23	5	1014	
2/24	12	1026	
2/25	14	1040	
2/26	14	1054	
2/27	1	1055	
2/28	10	1065	

March			
3/1	6	1071	
3/2&3	10	1081	
3/4	7	1088	
3/5	20	1108	
3/6	34	1142	Nueva Helvetia
3/24	16	1158	
3/25	18	1176	
3/26	21	1197	
3/27	42	1239	
3/28	17	1256	
3/29	8	1264	

April			
4/1	10	1274	
4/3	22	1298	
4/4	18	1314	
4/5	37	1351	
4/6	15	1366	
4/7	50	1416	
4/8	6	1422	
4/9	31	1453	
4/10	40	1493	
4/11	24	1517	
4/12	15	1532	
4/13	27	1559	Pass in Sierra
4/14	32	1591	
4/15	32	1623	
4/17	39	1662	
4/18	3	1665	
4/19	15	1680	
4/20	33	1713	Spanish trail
4/22	20	1733	
4/23	33	1766	
4/24	8	1774	
4/25	25	1799	
4/27	43	1854	
4/28	12	1854	
4/29	7	1861	
4/30	24	1885	

May			
5/1	15	1900	
5/2	12	1912	
5/3	18	1930	

5/4	57	1987
5/6	18	2005 Rio Virgen
5/7	10	2015
5/8	18	2033
5/9	1	2034
5/10	24	2058
5/11	12	2070
5/12	14	2084 Vegas San. Clara
5/13	15	2099
5/15	21	2120
5/16	17	2137
5/17	17	2154
5/19	27	2181
5/20	22	2203
5/21	31	2234
5/22	23	2257
5/23	12	2269 Sevier river
5/24	23	2292
5/25	32	2324
5/26	9	2333 Utah lake
5/27	22	2355

-- left Utah lake area --

INDEX